The flower-beds all were liberal of delight;
Roses in heaps were there, both red and white,
Lilies angelical, and gorgeous glooms
Of wall-flowers, and blue hyacinths, and blooms
Hanging thick clusters from light boughs; in short,
All the sweet cups to which bees resort,
With plots of grass, and leafier walks between
Of red geraniums, and of jessamine ...

Leigh Hunt 1784–1859

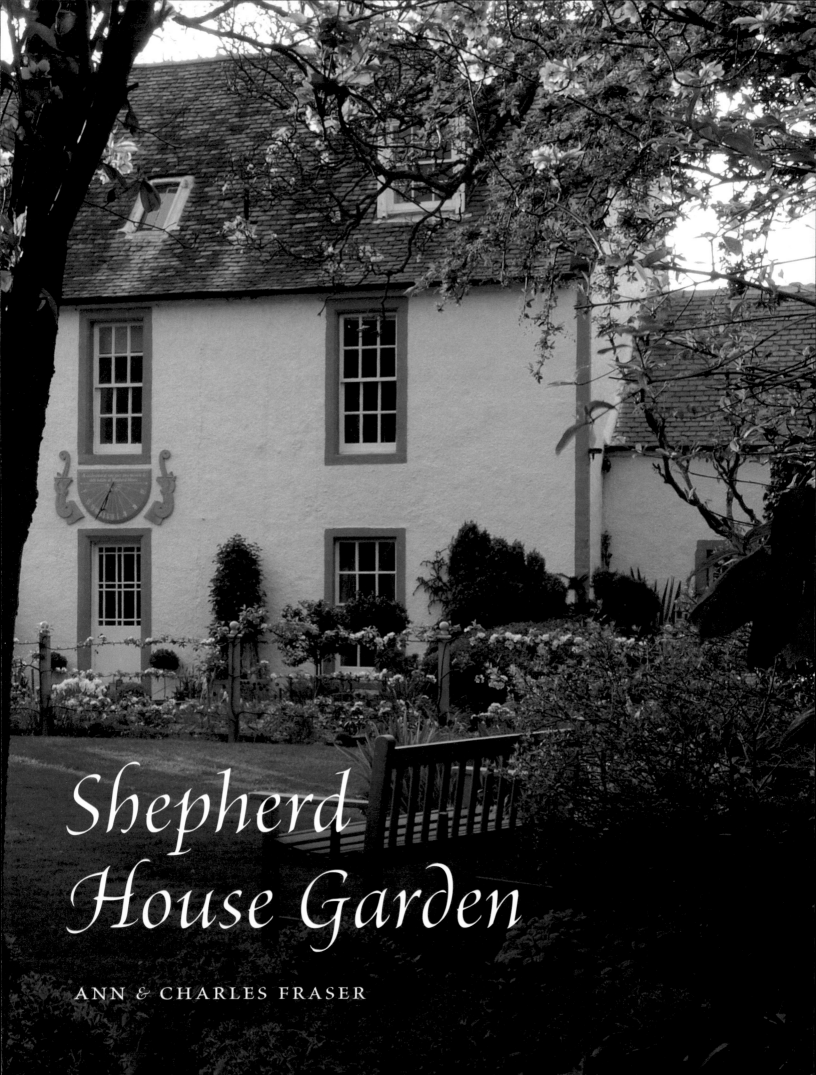

Shepherd
House Garden

ANN & CHARLES FRASER

SHEPHERD HOUSE
A VERY PERSONAL GARDEN

This book is dedicated
to all present and future gardeners
in our family.

First published in 2013 by Shepherd House Books
Shepherd House, Inveresk, East Lothian EH21 7TH

ISBN 978 0 9575649 0 9

Edited by Fay Young · Proofread by Hazel Reid
Designed and typeset in Brioni and Brioso by Dalrymple
Printed in Belgium by DeckersSnoeck

Frontispiece: looking across the centre of the garden,
towards Shepherd House, in the late afternoon sunlight.
Photo: Val Corbett

For garden opening times, contact numbers, information on paintings
and the holiday cottage please refer to www.shepherdhousegarden.co.uk
and also, for garden openings, www.scotlandsgardens.org

Contents

Foreword

In 2007, I embarked on an ambitious plan to write *Scotland for Gardeners*, a full-colour guide to Scotland's gardens, nurseries and all things horticultural with my photographer brother, Ray Cox. In two years we visited more than 500 gardens from Shetland to Galloway, and for both of us, Shepherd House was one of our highlights. From the famous rill to the wicker raised vegetable beds and the fleeting heads of the iris, visual treats abound round every corner. Shepherd House has featured in my lectures on Scottish gardens ever since.

I talked to hundreds of garden owners on my travels, and found that many gardens are the result of partnerships, usually somewhat unequal ones. Head gardener and labourer perhaps. At Shepherd House, however, I discovered a garden created by ideas, enthusiasm, hard work and design from both Ann and Charles. As each tells their story alternately throughout this book, the gardening partnership is revealed. Only occasionally you note a chord of disagreement. As Charles so eloquently puts it: 'She, the artist, has an eye for shape and colour that is absent in me, and her knowledge of plants is now profound. I like to get things done. Ann likes to get things right. We're a good team.'

Not everyone agrees what makes a good garden but for me it is usually a combination of good design and interesting plants. This pairing is perfectly illustrated at Shepherd House. This garden has evolved since 1957 and in common with most gardens, mistakes made in the early years formed part of the education that all the best gardeners go through.

The excellent photography in all the stages of this garden's existence and Ann's unique paintings of tulips, hellebores, irises and other plants, allow the reader to appreciate both the history of this garden and the detail. Above all, what this book illustrates so well is the process of gardening. Over many years everything grows or dies, thrives or struggles. Decisions are always needed and sometimes only the chainsaw will do. All gardening is evolution, never the same from season to season and year to year.

This beautifully illustrated book brilliantly captures two lifetimes in a very special garden. As Ann says: 'A shared journey, a combined passion ... central to our long happy marriage.'

KENNETH COX
Glendoick, January 2013

The potager in spring, Charlie's clipped box cones line the path. The four different varieties of pear trained on the arbour, blossom above mixed tulips and forget-me-nots.
PHOTO: VAL CORBETT

1   A Brief History of Inveresk

left *Seen from the air: Shepherd House and its one acre garden before all the conifers were removed. Garden visitors sometimes say the garden is 'paradise' and of course the meaning of this Persian word is 'walled enclosure'.*

right *A first glimpse of Shepherd House in 1957 before the road was widened. The front garden is still guarded by the two large sycamores now over 100 years old.*

[CHARLIE] What a cast of characters play out the plots of history in and around Inveresk: Romans, three major battles, Mary Queen of Scots, Cromwell, Bonnie Prince Charlie, even 'half hangit Maggie' (of whom more later). Few villages can have witnessed such a remarkable procession of characters and events.

The name Inveresk derives from two Gaelic words *inbhir* – at the mouth of – and *uisge* – water or river. Whisky derives from the same root as do the rivers Ouse and Usk. (There are four other rivers in the UK called Esk.) What is now known as the village of Inveresk is not at the mouth of the river but situated on a ridge overlooking the ancient burgh of Musselburgh which has grown over the centuries at the mouth of the river.

Perhaps the name suggests that in earlier times a far larger area than the present village was called Inveresk and the fact that the parish bears the name supports this view.

The Romans occupied the area from about the last quarter of the first century until they deserted Scotland in the middle of the fifth century. Early writers say surprisingly little about the Roman camp at Inveresk.

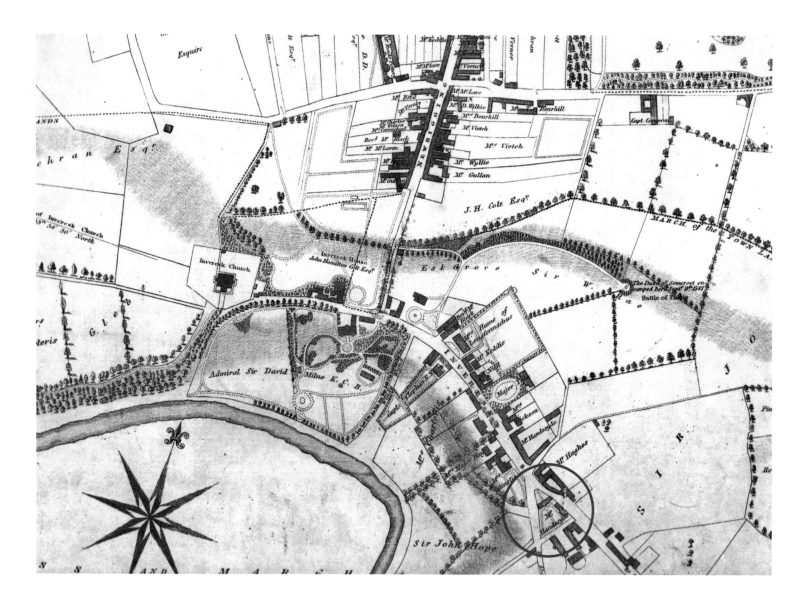

The triangular plot of Shepherd House (showing the central garden path) is clearly marked on a map of Inveresk from 1824.

Scarcely any archaeological digging had been undertaken perhaps because the 15th and 16th century cottages, and subsequently the larger houses, all discouraged excavation. The windows and doors of the early cottages can still be seen in the 10 ft garden walls, which are such a feature of the village. These, it is thought, were built from masonry robbed from the Roman buildings; experts can identify stones shaped by Roman masons with their diagonal chiselling.

The Roman Antiquities of Inveresk by D.M. Moir, 1860, provides an excellent account of what was then known of Roman Inveresk but since that was published much more has been discovered, particularly in recent years. It is now a usual condition of most planning permissions for development that a full archaeological survey is undertaken.

Little is known of post Roman Inveresk until the 16th century and from then onwards the area sees more than its share of the characters and events of history. The particularly bloody battle of Pinkie was fought in 1547 in the fields to the south of the village and it is said that the river ran red with blood for several days. The Duke of Somerset, who subsequently camped in the village (a stone marks the spot), had come in what was called the 'rough wooing' to persuade the Scots to marry their young Queen to the future Edward VI.

In 1567 the Battle of Carberry Hill took place and Mary Queen of Scots, surrendering to the rebel Lords, was led off to Edinburgh with Kirkcaldy of Grange, no doubt riding through the village. Her lover, the Earl of Bothwell, rode off to Dunbar and then to Denmark to a life of imprisonment. A stone on Carberry Hill shows where the tragic pair bade each other farewell.

In 1650 Oliver Cromwell, in his foray into the Lothians, made Inveresk House his headquarters and stabled his horses in the then church. There, it seems, he escaped an assassination attempt. The story is told in William Henry Langhorne's book *Reminiscences Connected Chiefly with Inveresk and Musselburgh* that in 1794 Robert Colt, the then proprietor of Inveresk House, made a gruesome discovery. During alterations to the house he removed some panelling, found a secret passage and there, under the room that Cromwell had occupied, was a mummified body of a cavalier in full armour with a keg of what appeared to be gunpowder.

Not far east of the village, the Battle of Prestonpans was fought in 1745 and a month or two later Langhorne's *Reminiscences* tell us that Bonnie Prince Charlie visited Inveresk House en route to Dalkeith on 1st November 1745.

What other village in Scotland has been so touched by the tides of history? And what of Shepherd House, sitting on the edge of the village and

Pole position: an unusual view of Shepherd House and garden taken by the tree surgeon Robin Wood from the top of the Wellingtonia before it was felled

From the rooftop: a view of the evolving garden.

across the road from Inveresk Lodge? Documents show the first conveyance or title of Shepherd House and its garden was in 1690 and the house was built about that time. Legend has it that it was built for a merchant who traded with the ports of the Hanseatic League and that may explain the curly gable, which does occur in Scotland but is more often found in the Netherlands and other North Sea ports.

A plan attached to the first title to the property in 1690 is precisely the plot of the present garden. It is said that an earlier house on the plot was the cottage in which the town herd or shepherd for Musselburgh lived. Hence the name of the house.

Each morning he would go down the hill to Musselburgh blowing his horn. From each close and vennel came cows, sheep, goats and pigs and the herd would lead them to the Burgh's common grazing, making sure that no harm came to them. In the evening the process would be reversed and each beast happily found the way back into its own byre. The title deeds from 1690 onwards tell us the names of owners but do not point to any well-known characters. One occupant during the early years of the 20th century was the distinguished artist Edwin Alexander RSA, RSW, RWS. Having spent his early life in Egypt, he married one of the Dott family of Aitken Dott (now The Scottish Gallery) and settled at Shepherd House. He painted mostly birds, butterflies, plants and animals in watercolour and reputedly kept a boa constrictor in one of the sheds, none of whose progeny have been found.

Queens and Princes, Dukes and Lord Protectors people the pages of Inveresk history and so does 'Half-Hangit Maggie'. Divorced by her husband in 1723, Maggie Dickson travelled south to Kelso, where she found work at the Inn at Maxwellheugh. There she got on the wrong side of the blanket with the innkeeper's son. She concealed the illegitimate pregnancy, then a capital offence. The baby was born prematurely and died soon after. She decided to put the body into the River Tweed but couldn't bring herself to do so and left it on the riverbank. Arrested and charged, she was convicted and hanged in the Grassmarket, Edinburgh. The body was cut down and wheeled to Musselburgh on a handcart for burial when noises were heard from within the coffin. The lid was lifted and there was Maggie still alive. Half-Hangit Maggie became something of a local celebrity and lived to a good age in one of the cottages in the village.

It is the hope of some of the residents that the village's future will be as illustrious as its past: but the threats are real. As they consider ever more planning applications, do the planning authorities appreciate that Inveresk is a unique example of an 18th century Scottish village?

The colours of Inveresk: an early watercolour painting by Ann, 1958.

2 Earliest Memories – Mughals & Manses

left *The garden at Bally House on the banks of the River Hoogley in Calcutta. Richly planted borders surround the Lutyens-esque pond.*

right *Maybe those early memories of Mughal gardens influenced us to build a rill at Shepherd House?*

[ANN: MUGHALS] I was born in India and spent the first nine years of my life there. India was a magical country for a child. We have been back on several occasions and as soon as I step off the plane the noise and smell of India bring happy memories flooding back.

My parents were both keen gardeners. Looking back, I realise that my father had a very strong sense of garden design. The garden he built at Bally House on the banks of the River Hoogley, Calcutta, was very Lutyens-esque in style and may even have been designed by Lutyens on the back of an envelope, as the great man's brother was a good friend of my parents and was in fact best man at their wedding in Calcutta. There were pools, fountains and pergolas and the garden was filled with tropical plants, birds and butterflies. Afternoon tea was taken under a magnificent

top left *The garden at Bally House, Calcutta, perhaps designed by Lutyens on the back of an envelope, was filled with tropical plants, birds and butterflies. Ann with her brother Robert sit on the back wall accompanied by their mother.*

top right *Ann with her brother Robert enjoying the cascade at Mughal Gardens of Nishat Bagh, Srinagar in 1942.*

centre *Graceful curves and low walls were striking features of the garden at Sunlaws, near Kelso designed by Ralph Hancock, for Ann's father.*

right *A page from our photo album: the magical Mughal gardens of Ann's childhood revisited in 1984.*

banyan tree. I can't remember all the plants that we grew except for lots of canna lilies and aromatic lantana bushes – their smell always reminds me of that wonderful garden. Cotton trees lined the riverbank and provided roosting sites for fruit bats.

Wages were cheap in India and in addition to countless gardeners my father employed a man especially to remove the dead bodies that the river washed up on our bank, some of them human. The man was paid per body removed. One day when walking round his garden my father recognised a body that had been removed the previous day. His smart employee had been removing bodies and taking them back up river to relaunch into the water, so being paid twice for the same body.

My brother and I were sent to school in Kashmir, a journey of three days and nights by train, in the company of our Scottish governess. The Garden School was started in 1935 for mainly British children of parents working in India. Situated in Srinagar during the winter, it transferred to Gulmarg at 9,000 ft in the foothills of the Himalayas in the summer. There are three Mughal gardens near Srinagar: Shalibar Bagh (abode of love), Nishat Bagh (abode of peace) and Chasmashahi (the royal spring) where Mughal emperors relaxed with their exquisite queens. They were wonderful places to explore as a child, when my parents rented a houseboat in the summer holidays on the Dal Lake, Srinagar, and my brother and I splashed in the fountains and slid down the cascades, the venue for

The 'canal zone' at Sunlaws (now the Roxburghe Hotel), in the Scottish Borders, photographed in the 1960s, with Simon, Ian and James amongst the azaleas.

many picnics. I can imagine that the fountains were only turned on for special occasions but these inspiring places sparked my interest in Mughal gardens. We revisited some of these wonderful gardens in 1984 before the troubles broke out in Kashmir. Sadly it is still a no – go area today.

After the death of my great uncle Brigadier General Robert Scott-Kerr in 1942, my father inherited the estates of Sunlaws and Chatto in the Scottish Borders near Kelso. When we returned from India in 1946 we came to live there. The large house (now The Roxburghe Hotel) was totally surrounded by *Rhododendron ponticum* bushes when we arrived and my father immediately had them removed. He then commissioned Ralph Hancock FRHS to design a garden. Wide graceful curves and low walls led the eye to the borrowed landscape beyond. Later my father himself designed what he called the canal zone (it was at the time of the Suez crisis): a series of ponds and streams planted with azaleas and primulas. I can't remember taking a great deal of interest in gardening at this stage of my life but I enjoyed the beauty of it and something evidently rubbed off.

Mansewood, Hamilton, Lanarkshire: a fine manse which had a large south facing garden leading down to the Cadzow burn.

[CHARLIE: MANSES] Ann and I visited Prince Charles's garden at Highgrove some years back. It is a delight. We were taken round in a group by an excellent guide. Fascinated by it all, I fell a little behind the rest of the party and spying an unusual plant I asked a passerby its name. 'I'm the sort of gardener who knows the names of the tools,' he replied. So do I and from quite an early age!

Ann and I both come from gardening families. Some day researchers will claim there is a gardening gene. In my case it could be traced back through four generations of the manse, a proud pedigree. Magnus Linklater phoned following the death of Gordon Brown, the then Prime Minister's father, a Church of Scotland minister. Magnus said he was writing an article about sons of the manse for *The Times* and asked me what it meant to be that. Off the top of my head I replied that it meant you came from a house full of books and that you were classless. He asked me for a few names of other sons of the manse and produced a typical light-hearted, clever article. By coincidence, the day the article appeared in *The Times* I met a distinguished cleric, also a son of the manse. I asked if he had seen the article and he replied that he sometimes thought that even if there were no God it would have been well worth inventing one so that Scotland could have sons of the manse.

Ministers used to live in fine manses with large gardens. My grandfather, The Rev. Charles Fraser had an impressive garden at the Manse of Croy, Inverness-shire. My father, The Very Rev. John Fraser, had equally impressive large gardens, first at Humbie in East Lothian and then at Hamilton in Lanarkshire. This latter garden was about three or more acres facing south leading to the Cadzow burn. Here I grew up, climbing the huge mature beech trees and sitting in rooks' nests (rather smelly) in the high treetops while the prevailing westerly winds gave a gentle sway to the branches. The evicted rooks greatly resented my visit to the treetops and loudly cawed their displeasure.

Father was the sort of gardener who logged in his diary: 'Strawberries first picked on 18th June, 2lbs' and 'Potatoes, first Earlies dug on 10th September – a good crop'. In these days parish ministers could afford gardeners and I remember Auld Jim Ramsay at Humbie and Myles at Mansewood, Hamilton. The latter was once found, rather the worse for wear, a long way from the manse and, asked his name by the local Bobby, he said he was Myles from Hamilton. The Bobby no doubt irritated said, 'Yes we know that, but what's your name?'.

War came in 1939, gardeners went. Father, having been a Gordon Highlander in the First World War, was in the army as a chaplain from day one of the Second World War until 1945. My sister was away at school, my mother and I struggled with the large garden; I guess it never recovered. I did 'Dig for Victory', produced row upon tidy row of vegetables and to this day have an inclination to grow plants in regimented lines. So, I certainly got to know the name of the tools, especially a fine push Ransome mower with which I cut the tennis lawn.

I also bred rabbits for the pot. These multiplied at an astonishing rate. I don't believe we ate a single one, but I quickly learned the facts of life. The rabbits died happy deaths, over-fed on my never-ending supply of 'Dig for Victory' vegetables. I also had then as I have now, a loft full of white fantail pigeons. The first pair I named Bill and Coo.

3   *Shepherd House & Garden*

left *Showing
the back of the house
and the position of the
courtyard garden.*
PHOTO: ANDREA JONES

right *The house in 1970
showing the Victorian
billiard room, which made
an excellent playroom (we
put the window in). Even
in the early days Charlie
had many fantail pigeons
to grace the lawn.*

[ANN: THE HOUSE]   When Charlie and I first saw Shepherd House in 1957, it was in poor shape. The house had been divided into two flats by two brothers and only the bottom flat was for sale.

However it suited our pockets at the time and even then it had a lot of charm. The garden was a wilderness and, like the house, divided in two. We met a young boy carrying a gun and when asked what he was shooting he replied 'RATS'. Luckily that didn't put us off and we moved in on return from our honeymoon. Two years later just before our first son was born we were able to buy the top flat.

Sadly, as was the custom of the 1950s and 60s all the old features of the house had been ruined, covered up or removed: fireplaces torn out and modern slab ones put in every room; panelled doors cut and lavatory glass installed or covered with hardboard. To get estimates for a new fireplace

above left Our first attempts at gardening: two formal beds of tulips planted between rose bushes in what is now the Courtyard garden in the 1960s.

above right Looking towards the house with its original colour of paintwork and showing what had been the entrance to the upper flat.

in the sitting room we went to Gray's Ironmongers in Edinburgh. 'Oh,' the man said, 'We know the house. When we were installing new fireplaces there we found three beautiful old mantelpieces lying in the garden.'

A decade or so later we discovered that underneath the plaster-board we had a stone staircase and after another decade, in two of the rooms upstairs, we found original panelling which has now been lovingly restored.

It has been a wonderful house for us as we were able to give each of our four sons a room to themselves and yet after they left we still seem to manage to occupy all the rooms.

In 1973 we converted what was the stable, pigeon loft and gardener's bothy into a separate cottage where we were able to accommodate my widowed mother for the last ten years of her life, after she had a stroke.

When we bought the house there was a rather ugly Victorian billiard room at the back of the house. It made an ideal children's playroom as it had a door into the garden. It also served as a village meeting place and

below left Simon in 1963. The central grass path was the first alteration we made.

below right Robert playing croquet with his cousin on the lawn, the scene of many family battles.

above left *The old stable, pigeon loft and bothy before we converted them into a separate cottage, where we were able to house my widowed mother for the last ten years of her life.*

above right *After alterations in 1974.*

on two occasions even a theatre. Jane Burnet, near neighbour and very good friend, and I formed a Children's Circle where all the children of the village met once a month to play games. An opera and a play were performed here, *Ruddigore* by Gilbert and Sullivan and *The Birthday of the Infanta* by Oscar Wilde. Heaven knows how we did it but they were well received. In 1984 after the playroom became redundant we took it down and built ourselves a conservatory.

[CHARLIE: THE GARDEN] Inveresk, as has been said, is on the site of a major Roman Camp, so I guess the land has been cultivated for more than two thousand years. The soil is neutral, deep and light, making it very easy to work. The climate is excellent for gardening. Average rainfall is around 20 inches a year, there is little frost and only in exceptional years do we get snow that lies for any length of time. The surrounding fields have a history of market gardening. Musselburgh leeks were once legendary. Now it is wall-to-wall barley.

below left *Robert in the back garden in 1974 aged four.*

below right *Robert aged five on his first day at Edinburgh Academy with his elder brothers: James 10, Ian 14 and Simon 16.*

The garden was a wilderness when we arrived. There was however a large lawn, which had never been cut, three large sycamores and five old apple trees. The whole plot is about an acre, an equilateral triangle 100 yards by 100 yards by 100 yards as can be seen on the plan.

Early on we went to the Scottish Record Office to see if there were old plans that would give us a clue as to what had been there before. We found that there had been a central path from the house up to the back wall. Restoring the path was the first structural thing we did. We also decided that we should plant some trees and asked Ann's father for his advice. Unfortunately, perhaps thinking of his estate at Sunlaws, he overestimated the size of our garden and recommended a Wellingtonia (or giant redwood), a blue cedar, a Scot's pine and several large conifers which were all far too big for our garden. This was one of many mistakes we made and 45 years later we have had to remove them all.

From the beginning I grew vegetables in tidy rows and as the garden was too big for our needs, I allowed our near neighbour Robin White to have a section. He was an agronomist which is perhaps why his cauliflowers and leeks grew much larger than mine but it was fun to deflate those who boasted of having a frightfully good gardener by responding that ours was an agronomist!

The garden was a playground for our four sons for 20 years although I continued to grow vegetables. I think it was when we decided to remove the old billiard room which had been the children's playroom and build a conservatory in its place, in 1984, that Ann's latent gardening gene awoke. And so over the years the garden has evolved.

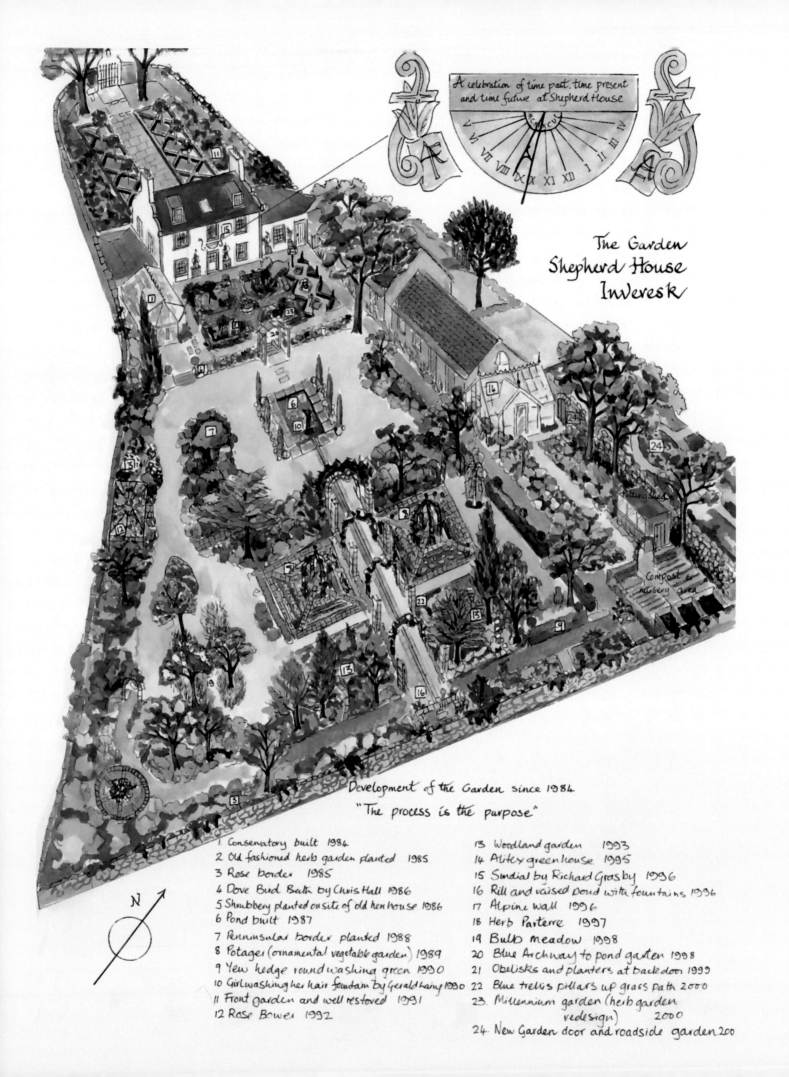

A celebration of time past, time present
and time future at Shepherd House

The Garden
Shepherd House
Inveresk

Development of the Garden since 1984

"The process is the purpose"

1. Conservatory built 1984
2. Old fashioned herb garden planted 1985
3. Rose border 1985
4. Dove Bird Bath by Chris Hall 1986
5. Shrubbery planted on site of old hen house 1986
6. Pond built 1987
7. Peninsular border planted 1988
8. Potager (ornamental vegetable garden) 1989
9. Yew hedge round washing green 1990
10. Girl washing her hair fountain by Gerald Laing 1990
11. Front garden and well restored 1991
12. Rose Bower 1992

13. Woodland garden 1993
14. Alitex greenhouse 1995
15. Sundial by Richard Grasby 1996
16. Rill and raised pond with fountains 1996
17. Alpine wall 1996
18. Herb Parterre 1997
19. Bulb meadow 1998
20. Blue Archway to pond garden 1998
21. Obelisks and planters at back door 1999
22. Blue trellis pillars up grass path 2000
23. Millennium garden (herb garden
     redesign) 2000
24. New Garden door and roadside garden 2001

N

4　Garden Design

[ANN] When we first came to live at Shepherd House we were so involved with getting the house in order and having a family that the garden was well down the list of things to do. There were few garden designers in those days and even if we had known of one and could have afforded one, we would not have been looking for their services. Recently garden designers have not had a very good name – by providing gardens like fitted kitchens they are destroying the magic of gardening.

We never had an overall design for the garden and had little knowledge of plants but by visiting other gardens we gradually got ideas of what we liked and what we wanted to create. For a garden to have meaning it must be personal. You either like it or you don't. Luckily the majority of our visitors seem to like it.

Our garden has evolved gradually over many years and each year we try to have a new project. If I could remake the garden I would not change it drastically, for I like its oddities. Nothing is symmetrical, there are not many right angles in the garden and nothing quite lines up – the central axis is not in line with the back door but very few people notice.

In a way the bones of the garden were already present with the high stone walls and also two different levels, which I think adds character. At first there was just a grassy bank dividing the areas and then we built the alpine wall with steps down and a path below it leading to the conservatory. I sometimes wonder about the curved borders as I think a formal framework should have straight lines but I have learnt to live with them.

The building of the rill, top pond and alpine wall, in 1996, was the largest project we have undertaken in the garden. But when that was done – rather like composing a painting – we felt the picture wasn't complete and needed a focal point at the house end of the vista. This led us to build the blue arch and to introduce the blue planters with their obelisks against the house. The right hand one thus became the focal point of the vista, looking back from the far end of the garden.

opposite *'The Process is the Purpose'. Plan of the garden drawn by Ann in 2000 giving dates of the all the garden projects. 'Nothing quite lines up – the central axis is not in line with the back door but very few people notice'.*

left *Before the alpine wall was built there was a grassy bank dividing the areas.*

right *The alpine wall and blue arch now in place, the old fashioned garden mostly planted with herbs including lavender, sage and rosemary begins to look distinctly blowsy in 1999. Ready for its revamp in the Millennium.*
PHOTO: JERRY HARPUR

below left *The courtyard garden in June 2007:* Phuopsis stylosa *in the foreground, growing in the double wall that surrounds this area with oriental poppy 'Pattie's plum' and Iris 'Quechee' behind.*

overleaf *To celebrate the Millennium we completely redesigned the courtyard garden and added many tulips and irises. In the central urn Ann usually plants the double early tulip 'Verona', beneath we have planted woodruff from where it can't escape! Other tulips 'Raspbery Ripple' foreground and 'Westpont' top right.*
PHOTO: VAL CORBETT

5 Courtyard Garden

left *Lily-flowered tulip 'Marilyn' together with 'Queen of the Night'.*

right *Looking down to the courtyard garden through the blue arch.*

[ANN] By 1985 our youngest son was 15 and away at school. Charlie has suggested that this is when my gardening gene awoke and certainly I now found new time for an interest which had probably always been there.

My love of gardens had started with the love of wild flowers. From an early age I knew the names of many wild flowers and later pressed, recorded and painted them. I was not encouraged to go to Art School as a student and was sent instead to Domestic Science College. In those days as an immature 17 year old you did what your parents wanted you to do! However, with our youngest son off at school, I enrolled as a mature student at Edinburgh College of Art for a four-year course in drawing and painting, followed by a course in botanical art at the Royal Botanic Garden Edinburgh. Gradually over the years new ideas emerged as I decided which plants I wanted to grow and which plants I enjoyed painting.

above left to right

The new conservatory built in 1984 to replace the old Victorian billiard room, looks out onto the newly planted garden which we then called 'The Old Fashioned Garden'.

Work in progress: preparing the ground for the new Millennium Courtyard Garden.

The new Courtyard Garden in full bloom in 2010.

The first area we designed – what we now call the Courtyard Garden – was immediately at the back of the house and very visible from the new conservatory. There was a vogue at the time for old plants and we planned to grow those that might have been growing in the garden during the 18th century. Having drawn our design we consulted a nursery called Plants from the Past and asked them to make a planting plan for us.

Like most people starting out along the garden trail we knew very little about plants so we were grateful for their advice. There were four beds divided by grass paths with a central bowl. We planted the beds with mostly old fashioned plants and herbs such as lavender, different varieties of sage, lots of violas, hyssop, thyme, old fashioned pinks, *Pulmonaria* and *Euphorbia*. At the centre of each bed we planted a standard Iceberg rose.

After 15 years the herbs had become woody and overgrown so to celebrate the millennium we completely re-designed this garden. We had started opening the garden for Scotland's Gardens Scheme and the grass paths had become worn by many visitors. We used old brick from a

left Having been told we would not be able to grow Rosa banksaie 'Lutea' we have proved the experts wrong. It flowers without fail in this sheltered corner.

top right 'The Herb Parterre' in December 2009, interplanted with cotton lavender, rue and lavender (planted in 1997).

right Snow adds an extra dimension, making magical patterns of the parterre in January 2010.

left *Oriental poppy 'Patties Plum' growing with* Iris *'Quechee' in the Courtyard Garden.*

right *The same combination in one of Ann's paintings.*
20 × 14 INCHES

fallen-down byre at the back of the garden to make herringbone paths.

The beds were dug over, manured and replanted using many of the same plants but this time I wanted to have each bed a different colour scheme: from mostly purples and pinks, to different shades of blues through whites and greys, with one bed mainly yellows.

By this time I had started painting plants so many irises and oriental poppies were included. A particular favourite combination which still exists today was oriental poppy 'Patty's Plum' with a wonderful brown iris called 'Quechee'. This plant combination I have painted several times. The beds also became a favourite place to plant the many different tulips, which I love to paint, keeping to the colour scheme. When we visited Helen Dillon's garden in Dublin she told us that she treated tulips as annuals. I certainly do not lift tulips except the ones planted in the permanent planters but I do add to them each year, sometimes varying the colour slightly. Certain tulips repeat very well in our dry garden soil, mainly the yellows (Jewel of Spring), whites (White Triumphator is particularly good) and reds (Jan Reus). To give more winter structure to the garden we replaced the standard Iceberg roses with four standard hollies.

The rose border was the next area we tackled. All the old shrubs came out. We had decided that we wanted mostly old shrub roses although we did choose some of David Austin's English roses. So with the help of numerous catalogues I drew a planting plan. Madame Hardy, Lordly Oberon, Queen of Denmark, Graham Thomas, Cardinal de Richilieu, Proud Titania and Charles Austin were amongst the 40 roses we selected. I love to think of them all having conversations. We also commissioned our friendly blacksmith to build a rose arbour and planted pink roses to clamber over it: Blush Noisette, Constance Spry, Blush Rambler and Debutante.

Pink roses, 'Blush Noisette', 'Constance Spry', 'Blush rambler' and 'Debutante' cover the rose arbour in July.
PHOTO: VIVIAN RUSSELL

overleaf

left *Ann's painting of the parrot tulip 'Flaming Parrot' with* Aquilegia canadensis.
20 × 14 INCHES

right *Ann's painting of the parrot tulip 'Black Parrot' with* Allium aflatunense
20 × 14 INCHES

Tulipa 'Flaming Parrot' Aquilegia formosa   May 2005 Ann Fraser

Ann's painting of mixed
tulips all grown in the garden
at Shepherd House.

22 × 29 INCHES

Ann Fraser 2011

6 Front Garden

left *The parterre is a fitting formal entrance to the house. Criss-crossing box hedges interplanted with standard Iceberg roses create an illusion of symmetry.*
PHOTO: ANDREA JONES

right *A view from the front gate guarded by the sycamore trees, throwing their friendly shadows across Shepherd House.*
PHOTO: VIVIAN RUSSELL

[CHARLIE] Guarded by two large sycamore trees, the front gate is at the north corner of the plot. The sycamore trees are over a hundred years old and are quite a feature of the village. Strangely one bursts into leaf a week or so before its neighbour and in the autumn loses its leaves a week or so earlier.

In 1957 there were two conifers in patches of grass on either side of a gravel path to the front door. As there is no access front to back other than through the house, it was a nuisance to bring tools from one to the other and after some years a lower maintenance garden seemed wise.

In 1991 Ann came up with a design using criss-crossing box hedges which would make the plots look more symmetrical (though nothing in this garden is symmetrical). The area in between the hedges was

The newly planted box parterre in 1991.

filled with gravel and standard Iceberg roses were planted in each of the three squares on either side of the path. Two yew trees lean against the house. The paving is treated once a year with weedkiller (Pathclear), the box hedges trimmed in July and the yew in September. There is no such thing as a low maintenance garden but our front garden now needs less maintenance.

[ANN] Box hedging, parterres and knot gardens, first used in the Renaissance gardens of the 16th century, were coming back into fashion in the 1980s and 1990s, partially inspired by Rosemary Verey's garden at Barnsley House in Gloucestershire.

Eight years later the parterre is flourishing and box hedging neatly clipped.

Box parterres make a good formal entrance to the house; great to look down on from upstairs and they give the impression of being neat and tidy all year round. They look even better in winter when they are sometimes covered with frost or snow accentuating the geometric shapes of the design.

One of the many advantages of this house is that there is a view of the garden from every window so we are able to look down on the parterres both front and back.

Snow accentuates geometric shapes of the formal front garden.

7 Centre of the Garden

left *Looking down
the garden path:
Camellia × williamsii
'Jury's Yellow' flourishes
against the wall, very
often flowering as early
as February.*

PHOTO: SHEILA SIM

right *Borrowed views:
the Nepeta Walk, inspired
by Tyninghame House
Gardens, runs the length
of the rill, which was
inspired by a visit to the
Generalife Gardens at
the Alhambra.*

[ANN] For the first 20 years of our life at Shepherd House the main
lawn was much in use as a football, rugby, tennis, cricket and croquet
pitch. But once the family had grown up we started to reclaim the garden
from the children! As we didn't have an overall plan we took it one bit at
a time.

Having redesigned the Courtyard Garden and Rose Border our next
project was to make a formal pond (we had already made an informal
pond out of the duck pond in the old hen run). We widened the existing
grass path and, inspired by the Nepeta Walk at Tyninghame, East Lothian,
lined either side of the path with Nepeta. We commissioned the local
blacksmith to make four wide cast iron arches over which we planted
white rambling roses (Bobby James, Wedding Day and Seagull) as well as
various clematis. The new pond was positioned in line with the grass path

The June garden:
lupins, oriental poppies
'Coral Reef', with Rosa
californica plena *behind*.

but of course it wasn't central to the lawn. To overcome this we dug a new border which we called the peninsular border. We now had horseshoe shaped borders with a central formal pond.

My original colour scheme for the borders was to start with the brightest colours in the sunniest position and keeping to the colour wheel (newly learnt at art college) take a clockwise direction gradually ending up with blues and purples. This makes decisions much easier when placing new plants in the border. Of course colour schemes don't

always work. Self-seeders do not understand colour schemes and I rarely have the heart to pull out a plant that has seeded in the wrong place.

Other areas we planted about this time were a shrubbery along the back wall of the garden where there was an old byre. Greatly helped by the now teenage sons we demolished the byre which had been our hen house and used the old brick to make a herringbone path along the front of the new shrubbery. In those days we rarely could afford professional help and just piled compost on top of the remaining hen house rubble (which still makes planting in this area extremely difficult).

Several years later we visited the Alhambra in Spain. Inspired by the rills and the Generalife Gardens we came home determined to construct a rill to run from a raised pond at the back wall of the garden, down the grass path to the formal pond. Nine years later in 1996 the rill was built!

At first we commissioned an expert on water gardens to produce plans.

The fountain and pond
framed by a blue arch
adorned with Rosa
'Ghislaine de Feligonde'.

above, left to right

The garden takes shape; the Nepeta Walk before the rill was built.

The new formal pond dug by hand by Jasmine Cann. The pond in spring lined with Tulip 'White Triumphator', also showing the six Cupressus arizonica 'Fastigiata' *trees that grew too big for their space.*

Jack Gilmour, who had helped us with hard landscaping, thought the designs were overly complicated and that much of what was proposed was unnecessary. So Jack undertook all the building, electrical and plumbing work and made an excellent job. Water is recycled underground to a tank at ground level at the far end; from here it is pumped into the raised pond through four jets hidden in four bowls of hostas. The rill drops just one inch in all its 40ft length so it was important to get the levels exactly right, and Jack did.

My favourite reference book about this time was *Classic Garden Design* by Rosemary Verey. I became a tremendous fan of her garden at Barnsley which inspired us to create our next project: a potager garden. In fact we made two identical potagers on either side of the grass path and in the centre of each we asked our friendly blacksmith to make two arbours up which we could train pears. It was very much in vogue at the time to create garden rooms and with this in mind we planted a yew hedge round what had been our drying green.

right *Changing seasons reveal different moods of the garden. Blue structures stand out and the rill marks a bold line through the snow.*

below right *In spring the fountain is reflected in the rill.*

Gerald Laing's fountain of a girl washing her hair: Six pillars of clipped beech underplanted with Iris 'Blue Rhythm' *surround the pond, with* Rosa californica plena *behind shaped bushes of yellow privet.*

The climax of the garden, usually at the end of June or early July, when the roses on the arches come into bloom. 'Bobby James', 'Wedding Day' and 'Seagull' contrast with the blue of Nepeta *'Six Hills Giant'*

above left *A painter's palette of plants. 'Jan Reus' with other hot coloured tulips contrast
with the beech pillars beyond, still with their coppery winter foliage.*

left *Oriental poppies 'Coral Reef' growing in front of* Euphorbia cornigera.

above *Newly planted in 2012;* Hebe rakaiensis *interplanted with* Allium albopilosum
'Christophii' *echoing the rounded shape of the* Hebe.

One of Ann's favourite compositions of the black Iris *'Superstition'*
and white oriental poppies, 'Black and White'.
20 × 28 INCHES

Painting of mixed oriental poppies
all grown in the garden at Shepherd House.
22 × 29 INCHES

8 Art & Structure

left *The blue planter with obelisk and bird feeder catch the eye. All the woodwork in the garden is painted the same soft shade of blue. The climbing rose in the planter is again* Rosa *'Ghislaine de Feligonde'.*

right *A bronze resin cock and hen among spring Crocus 'Vernus Vanguard' in the wild garden.*

[ANN] Our garden is full of memories of good friends and family, not only through the plants they have given us over the years but also through the works of art and interesting bits and pieces we have been given or purchased.

It is the architectural elements – arbours, pergolas, arches, fountains, urns, paths, trees, hedges, clipped shrubs, even benches – that give the garden its character. We have chosen to paint all the wooden structures in the garden a soft shade of grey/blue (Sadolin Superdec 'Limestone'). All this adds an extra dimension to the garden and makes it more interesting to look at and more exciting to explore.

The first piece of work we commissioned was the Dove Bird Bath by Chris Hall. Chris had worked on the Abbey Cloisters on Iona and is well regarded. The dove is made of soft stone which suffers in our hard climate but fortunately Chris has been able to repair it for us. The birdbath was

A pair of mallard ducks
disturb the reflection of
Gerald Laing's fountain of
the girl washing her hair.

A pair of mallard ducks
disturb the reflection of
Gerald Laing's fountain of
the girl washing her hair.

chiselled out of an enormous rock that Chris single-handedly brought
into the garden.

The sundial on the house was a gift presented when Charlie retired as
Deputy Chairman of United Biscuits. The artist was Richard Graseby who
lives in the south of England and the sundial travelled north in the boot
of our youngest son Robert's car.

The bronze fountain of the girl washing her hair in our pond is by our
good friend Gerald Laing. Sadly, he died in November 2011 at the age of 76.
Famous for his pop art and public sculpture, Gerald will be greatly missed
but luckily we have a constant reminder of his friendship and talent.

All the urns, bowls and obelisks are from Haddonstone or other manufacturers. The owl sitting on top of a felled tree we had carved by a chain saw sculptor. The tulip seat carved out of the stump of the Wellingtonia is by Robin Wood, a local artist whose chainsaw has also been put to work in the garden to fell overlarge or damaged trees.

What we call our fank (Scots for sheep pen) or 'sitooterie' was built by Nigel Bialy of Dry Stone Designs as was the potting shed. Dry stone walling is fast becoming a lost art which is a great shame but true craftsmen like Nigel achieve remarkable results. No cement was used in our structures except in the potting shed where the walls are set in a lime/cement mortar on the inside while leaving a dry stone exterior.

A carved owl sitting on top of a tall tree trunk covered with Clematis montana *'Rubens'.*

The sundial by Richard Graseby, a retirement gift to Charlie.

Nigel uses local stone gathered from fields after ploughing. We wanted a 'living roof' and as it was a shady area chose to plant a species of fern suitable for dry shade (*Polypodium vulgare*) which has been very successful although the only way to weed it is to crawl about on the roof on your hands and knees!

The Alpine Wall, copied from the Royal Botanic Garden Edinburgh, was built at the same time as the rill by a skilled dry stone waller. The stone was acquired from a quarry at Crichton in exchange for a case of whisky!

All the cast iron supports including the rose arbour were made by our friendly blacksmith at Drem with whom we have sadly lost touch.

We have recently become friendly with Andrea Geile and have

right Viola, Erigeron karvinskianus, *and* Campanula *tumble over the alpine wall built at the same time as the rill.*
PHOTO: JERRY HARPUR

below right *The Potting Shed built by Nigel Bialy with native fern* Polypodium vulgare *growing on the roof.*

opposite *The fank or sitooterie also built by Nigel Bialy of Dry Stone Design.*
PHOTO: ANDREA JONES

purchased many of her works of art (often serving a dual purpose as plant supports) which she makes in oxidised steel. Recently she has been coming to sell her art at our garden openings. The bronze resin cock and hen in the wild garden were purchased from the RSA summer exhibition as a birthday present for Charlie and the bronze pigeons came from Whytock and Reid.

The wooden archway at the top of the steps came from a kit and like all

left *Two tulip mosaics designed by Maggie Howarth, the doyenne of pebble mosaic art.*

right *Metal art by Edinburgh-based artist Andrea Geile.*

the wooden structures is painted a soft shade of blue. At the same time, having seen the espaliered crab apples at Alnwick we constructed a low fence between the Courtyard Garden and the Main Garden in order to train *Malus* 'Red Sentinel'. Crab apples are such good value as not only do you get the spring blossom but in the winter the cordon is studded with small bright red apples that resemble Christmas decorations. The crab apples last well into the New Year and only once they have been softened by frost will they be stripped from the branches by blackbirds.

My 70th birthday present from Charlie was three tulip mosaics commissioned from Maggy Howarth, the doyenne of pebble mosaic designers.

Our next project is to build a Shell House and we have already asked Lachlan Stewart of Anta Architecture to produce some drawings for us (as I write, they are with East Lothian planning department). He designed the Shell House for the Queen Mother's Garden at the Royal Botanic Garden Edinburgh.

There is always something new to look forward to. We find that the most exciting thing about creating a garden is the next project.

The top pond surrounded by white Abutilon *and the Ostrich fern* Matteuccia struthiopteris. *Fountains spout from urns of green and white hostas.*

*The top pond in spring with hostas just emerging: other plants, from left to right, include
the wonderfully scented* Osmanthus burkwoodii, Hydrangea petiolaris *climbing through the
rampant ivy at the back of the pond and* Piptanthus nepalensis *on the right.*
PHOTO: VAL CORBETT

A Man's Compost Heap
Is His Castle

9 The Art of Making Compost

[CHARLIE] My art form is composting. Above the four large compost boxes, inscribed on a piece of Caithness slate are the words 'A man's compost heap is his castle'. So the compost heaps are mine and I happily share them with the hens.

All that rots ends up in the bins. Leaves, grass cuttings spread in layers of about two inches thick and green garden waste – all go into the bins. But twigs and branches are not allowed and nor are weeds if they are showing signs of seeding. Those that spread with such success through their root system, such as bishop's weed and bindweed (*Convolvulus)* are definitely excluded. Droppings swept from the floor of the hen house and pigeon loft are welcome, as is ash from the bonfire.

Kitchen waste is not added to the brew but put for two or three months into a revolving compost maker to which Mr Rat, if he is about, cannot gain access. The contents are added to the bins when truly rotted.

When each of the boxes is nearly full I add a layer of mature compost. I wonder why? Perhaps it is because it just looks so much better, but my belief is that it seals in whatever heat is generating in the box and also it brings colonies of earth worms and other compost making partners into immediate action. When the compost is mature, usually by October, we dig out the boxes and spread the contents round the garden.

Thus we make enough, or nearly enough, compost for our needs. We do buy in supplies of John Innes for seed planting and potting up, and with such deliveries we order sacks of bone meal and the fertiliser Growmore. The potting shed and greenhouse usually have Magic-gro to hand, a growth-promoter strongly recommended by Robin Lane Fox in his excellent book *Thoughtful Gardening*. Kind neighbours allow me to barrow in loads of horse manure and every three or four years we mulch the whole garden with mushroom compost.

We certainly don't claim to know all the answers to composting but it plays an invaluable role in adding moisture, texture and nourishment to the light, dry soil in our garden. However there is always more to learn about any art; like my school reports I'm sure we are capable of doing better.

opposite *All that rots ends up in the bins: one of Charlie's four compost boxes which he happily shares with the hens.*

10 Wild & Woodland Gardening

left *The wonderfully strong growing* Trillium kurabayashii *behind a double white hellebore.*

right *Winter aconites* (Eranthis hyemalis), *the spring snowflake* (Leucojum vernum), *snowdrops and crocus.*

[ANN] The title suggests we have acres of wild woodland. In fact about a quarter of our garden is given over to less formal planting of trees, shrubs, bulbs and wild flowers. There is a different atmosphere in this part of the garden which I rather like.

Thirty years after we had planted all the trees towards the back of the garden, as advised by my father, many of them had outgrown their space. The temporary solution was to cut their skirts off and plant a woodland garden underneath. However it soon became obvious that more radical action was needed and year-by-year we started felling one large tree after another.

Out came most of the conifers: Scots pine, Thuyas, the Wellingtonia and six *Cupressus arizonica* 'Fastigiata' which we had planted round the pond hoping they would stay slim like the wonderful Italian cypresses.

They didn't and have been replanted by six clipped pillars of beech.

Three magnolias have survived the cull: a white *Magnolia soulangeana* which grew to 30ft or more then suddenly died right back but is now sprouting from the base; *Magnolia kobus* which also grows enormous (we will probably live to regret it) and *Magnolia* × 'Elizabeth' one of the first ever yellow magnolias, which we associate with Betty Scholtz of Brooklyn Botanic Garden – our young tree was given to us and brought to Shepherd House in a suitcase by an American friend.

As we became more knowledgeable about trees and how big they grow, we gradually added some choice smaller trees to our collection. I have always admired *Prunus serrula* for its wonderful peeling, shiny, coppery brown bark; with the sun behind it in the winter it looks as if it is on fire. In the very early years I bought a tree from Woolworths which turned out to be *Sophoro japonica* or Japanese Pagoda Tree. It is now 30ft tall and although it has never flowered we are still hopeful as we have read that it can take 30 years to bloom. You have to be patient with trees but it pays off as our *Davidia involucrata* (handkerchief tree) and *Liriodendron tulipifera* (tulip tree), both bought over 15 years ago, are now flowering regularly.

We have a growing collection of American dogwoods which flower extremely well. *Cornus* 'Eddies White Wonder' is a star and always puts on a show for our May garden openings with its display of huge creamy white flowers and this autumn its leaves have turned a wonderful strawberry colour. *Cornus alternifolia variegata* (the wedding cake tree) creates quite a show all summer. We also have the spring flowering *Cornus mas* which gives a very long period of interest. From February onwards, when the sweet smelling small yellow flowers appear on bare twigs, this *Cornus* puts on a great display. In the autumn it has good leaf colour as well as bright red cherry-like fruits which are edible although we have never been tempted to try them.

We have only managed to grow one Japanese maple, *Acer palmatum* 'Sango-kaku', which has stunning autumn colour. We have tried on several occasions to grow others but failed maybe because it was too dry or windy although being a walled garden you would have thought otherwise. However we now have two snake bark acers which I love. *Acer davidii* 'George Forrest' has red and grey striated bark and bright red young growth; it also has good autumn colour so is an excellent all round tree. The other snake bark, which is quite new, is *Acer tegmentosum* 'Joe Witt'. It has bright white striated bark and promises to be a stunning tree.

Many years ago we planted three different species of *Eucryphia* and they have taken a very long time to flower well but now put on a good autumn show. The only name that I remember is *Eucryphia* × *nymansensis*

previous pages, clockwise from left

The wild tulip Tulipa sylvestris *and* Fritillaria meleagris *flourish in the wild garden.*

The modern shrub rose 'Nevada' and Epimedium *growing under the 'Woolworth tree'. The rose is at its best in May when the arching branches are covered with large creamy white flowers.*

Rhododendron *'Loderi King George' is one of the few rhododendrons to survive in our neutral soil with the help of generous helpings of iron. Pink buds open to large trusses of sweetly scented flowers. On the other side of the path is* Paeonia mascula *the wild peony.*

Fragrant white Narcissus *'Thalia' surrounds a traditionally made pot from Crete.*

right, clockwise from left

The Handkerchief Tree Davidia involucrata *rewarded us for our patience after fifteen years and now flowers regularly in May and June.*

Magnolia × *'Elizabeth' having been brought to us in a suitcase is now thirty feet tall. It has luminous pale yellow flowers in early spring. Few species can match the elegant drama of it in full bloom.*

Cornus × *'Eddies White Wonder' with huge creamy white bracts is a star and always puts on a show for our May garden openings.*

We have three different forms of Eucryphia, *this one was flowering as late as December 2012.*

left, clockwise from top

The bulb garden with mostly white Narcissus *and* Fritillaria *in April. On right of grass path* Erythronium 'Pagoda' *grows in perfusion.*

The giant Himalayan lily Cardiocrinum giganteum *grows up to three metres. It is monocarpic (it flowers, sets seed and dies) but there are usually two or three smaller bulbils waiting to take its place the following year.*

Charlie walking through the woodland garden.

Orchids growing in the wild garden are at last beginning to spread.

which was covered in white flowers in September; the other two are smaller but one is still flowering as I write in mid November.

All the trees have been underplanted with various choice plants to give the area a woodland feel: ferns, hellebores, trilliums, anemones, cyclamen, tulips, epimediums and of course snowdrops.

The old orchard still had three of the original old apple trees. Sadly, we lost one in the winter gales but have now replaced it with a Cox's orange pippin. Some years ago we decided to plant a bulb and wild flower garden in this area and it has been very successful. The area starts flowering in February with species crocus, and then goes on to fritillaries, *Narcissus* (mostly white) *Camassia, Chinodoxa, Scilla*, many species tulips and then wild flowers. In fact wild flowers are notoriously difficult to get going but we now have meadow cranesbill (*Geranium pratense*) as well as campions, buttercups, daisies, leopard's bane (*Doronicum*) and are delighted that the cowslips are now multiplying and doing well.

In 2012 for the first time I planted the almost black 'Queen of the Night' tulips (as they do at Highgrove) and they successfully fill the gap between earlier bulbs and wild flowers. We don't cut the area until the end of August.

'Queen of the Night' tulips growing in the wild garden in May, filling the gap between Narcissus, Fritillaria *and summer's wild flowers.*

Watercolour painting by Ann of some of the plants growing in the wild garden.

20 × 28 INCHES

11 Vegetable Garden

left *Watercolour portrait of beetroot by Ann.*
18 × 12 INCHES

right *Raised beds bordered by woven willow created in 2010 are excellent for growing salads.*

[CHARLIE] As bit-by-bit the garden developed so the area for vegetables has been moved around. The original site in the far part of the garden was more than a patch. As the family reduced in numbers, as son by son left for university, the vegetables were moved to the newly constructed potager.

A potager is a French word for ornamental kitchen garden. Having seen the garden at Barnsley House and Villandry, I planned to grow vegetables for their shape and colour rather than their taste. This didn't work. For example, a row of Webb's Wonderful lettuces, each plant interspersed with Lola Rossi, looked wonderful until we ate a couple and then the whole design looked like a mouth with missing teeth.

So in disgrace the vegetables were moved after a year or two to an area near to the garden entrance, beside the greenhouse and potting shed.

below *Full to over-
flowing: later in the year
the beds become very
productive.*

That seemed to make gardening sense. Ann designed a series of raised
beds each bordered by woven willow with tall willow wands forming a
dividing archway up which we grow runner beans.

This all looks good but the jury (i.e. me) is still out. Despite having
lined the woven willow with plastic material, how long will it last? These

raised beds in an already dry garden are dryer and need regular summer
watering. The soil is still loose which perhaps accounts for beetroot and
leeks shooting at an early stage in their growth.

We grow only autumn raspberries and one row of early potatoes. The
pear trees produce a succession of gorgeous pears; the plum tree in a good
year fills baskets of fruit, picked before the wasps attack.

opposite *An eye for
detail in the vegetable
garden: climbing runner
beans grow on wands of
willow and the arches line
up with a hole in the yew
hedge beyond.*

Later in the year the potager becomes a colourful mix of flowers mostly grown from seed: cosmos, cornflowers, marigolds, Lavatera, Agapanthus and poppies.

Meantime, the so-called potager, having said farewell to the vegetables is now home to annuals, which produce great colour later in the year, cosmos, marigold, cornflower and whatever seed packet grabs my attention as I study the seed catalogues.

Iris unguicularis and *Galanthus elwesii*   Ann Fraser 2012

12 Plants & Painting

left Iris unguicularis *'Mary Ballard' with* Galanthus elwesii *painted by Ann especially for the book on Greywalls house and garden, published in March 2013.*
16 × 12 INCHES

right *Ann in her studio painting a selection of brown and yellow irises.*
PHOTO: VIVIAN RUSSELL

[ANN] People often ask which came first, the garden or the painting and I find that difficult to answer. I have always wanted to paint but when I enrolled at Edinburgh College of Art I did not know exactly what type of painting that I would end up doing so I began with a four year general course. I then went on for a further year to study at the Royal Botanic Garden Edinburgh (RBGE), where the course in botanical painting was run in conjunction with the art college. My tutors were John Mooney and Paul Nesbit (unfortunately I missed the first year when Elizabeth Blackadder had been the tutor). At the time Rory McEwen had a retrospective exhibition at Inverleith House curated by Paul Nesbitt. I was greatly encouraged when Paul asked if he could buy a painting I had done of a *Fritillaria* for his mother. Paul was an excellent teacher and suggested that I should paint tulips. I have been in love with them ever since.

above *'Delphiniums' painted by Ann, all grown in the garden at Shepherd House.* 23 × 29 INCHES

below *Delphiniums need to be well staked so as not to be shattered by summer gales.*

I joined The Wakefield Tulip Society, an old florist society dedicated to growing and showing the English Florists' Tulip. These beautiful tulips are distinguished by flamed and feathered markings caused by Tulip Breaking Virus, highly valued during the 17th century tulipomania. Because of the virus these tulips are not commercially available so the only way to obtain bulbs is by joining the society. Unfortunately they need specialised treatment and although I was reasonably successful to begin with it didn't last.

I'm glad to say my first solo show in London in 1991 at the Malcolm Innes Gallery was very successful and since then I have exhibited widely in Edinburgh and London. The Royal Horticultural Society has awarded me three medals for my botanical art: Silver in 1989, Silver Gilt in 1993 and Gold Medal in 2009. Dr Shirley Sherwood purchased one of my paintings from a London Show. She is a wonderful patron of the botanical artist, exhibiting her collection all round the world including the Smithsonian Museum in Washington. She has also published several books on her collection and has now built a gallery at Kew Gardens so she can put her collection on permanent display.

In 2011 I was asked to do a solo show at the Tryon Gallery in London. I exhibited 40 paintings and was relieved that half of them sold, as the large paintings take me a month or more to complete. In fact all the large complex multi-plant portraits sold and the gallery asked for some more for a mixed exhibition in 2012. I always have an idea of what colours I want in the paintings and sometimes do little sketches of the key plants. Having drawn the flowers, I then arrange them on the page as if they are growing in the garden. The flowers are painted first followed by the stems and leaves, depending upon the interrelation of the heads. Having built up the under painting in layered washes of diluted colour I sketch in the folds and shadows gradually building up the deeper colours until I feel they are utterly convincing.

Painting plant portraits is the best way to get to know a flower in all its moods, in all the stages of its development, and also its scent. I am not a botanist or an illustrator but I do have a passion for plants and paint them as I see them even if a petal has withered or if there is slug damage.

Painting Tulips

Top of the list for me is the tulip: from a tight green bud which promises so much, yet gives nothing away as to its final colour, to the large cupped flower on a strong straight stem; as it matures, petals fall outwards revealing dark anthers, relinquishing its neat shape. Tulips come in all colours (except true blue) and sizes. Some are frilled and lacerated, some are gaudily streaked and striped, some have pointed reflexed petals like a lily and others have a neat rounded form.

Tulips 'Queen of the Night', 'Negrita', 'Shirley' and 'Caravelle'   Ann Fraser 2011

left *Watercolour painting by Ann of single late tulips; 'Queen of the Night', 'Shirley' and 'Caravelle'.*
20 × 14 INCHES

above *Similar tulips growing in the garden in 2011.*

right, clockwise *Tulips 'Apricot Parrot', broken tulip and 'Queen of the Night'.*

Black and white tulips 'Queen of the Night', 'Spring Green', 'White Parrot', broken tulip and 'Maureen', a watercolour painting by Ann.
20 × 28 INCHES

In the garden at Shepherd House we have tulips flowering from the end of February until the beginning of June. The first to come out are the bright red species tulips, which open their petals on sunny days. These we have planted in the iris border as they enjoy the same hot and dry conditions. We have tiny alpine tulips, some only a few inches tall which also like hot and dry conditions. The alpine and species tulips flower well year after year, but the later larger tulips need to be replenished regularly. The later tulips I plant in large groups to blend in with the surrounding foliage. Forget-me-nots make very satisfactory companions, complimenting the colour of the tulips.

Painting Irises

As with tulips, artists have been inspired to paint irises for centuries. They have a haunting scent and perfectly balanced shape where the three central petals (standards) stand up and the three outer ones (falls) curve down. The falls and standards can be different colours or different shades

of the same colour. They can be frilled or ruffled along the edges or their petals might be stippled or etched with a deeper shade. The colour range is immense but thankfully as yet includes no true scarlet.

I have also frequently painted the winter flowering *Iris unguicularis*. It flowers so unexpectedly, usually in February or March, brightening dark corners on winter days. It is very good for picking and has a wonderful scent. Picking in bud and watching it unfurl its petals is a joy. In fact I have chosen this iris to paint specially for a recent commission by Roy McGregor of Gullane Art Gallery who has asked me to contribute some paintings of plants for a book he is writing about Greywalls Hotel in Gullane, East Lothian. Gertrude Jekyll designed the garden for the house built by Sir Edwin Lutyens. She also painted the winter iris (in those days its botanical name was *Iris stylosa*) which she had seen growing in its native home when she was exploring the rocky hills of Algeria. Miss Jekyll was careful to place it in her gardens at the foot of sunny walls to continue her theme of soft colouring into the depths of winter.

Watercolour painting of the English Florist Tulip 'Rory McEwen'. Rory was the patron of the Wakefield Tulip Society until his untimely death in 1982.
10 × 14 INCHES

Mixed tall bearded irises growing in front of the pale green, newly emerged foliage of the wisteria.

The tiny alpine varieties flower so fleetingly that you have to be constantly vigilant to spot them. Next come the dwarf irises, the intermediates and the exquisite *Iris florentina*, the emblem of the city of Florence. But the real drama comes with the tall bearded iris. They are best planted in a bed on their own as they do not like having their rhizomes covered. They are a lot of work as they really should be divided every four or five years but I wouldn't be without them. They flower best in hot dry conditions which sadly Scotland cannot always provide, however we have them along the whole length of the cottage interplanted with early tulips and that seems to work. They are heavy feeders so I treat them to a general purpose fertiliser (Growmore or Rose fertiliser seems to keep them happy).

Most of my irises are blue, yellow, brown or purple so last year I decided to introduce a new colour and ordered a selection of Cedric Morris Irises otherwise known as Benton Irises. A friend of Vita Sackville-West, the

The mid season tall bearded iris 'Blue Rhythm' a wonderful cornflower blue and a strong growing iris, beside the pond

creator of Sissinghurst, Sir Cedric Morris was an artist who not only painted irises but bred them. He spent years refining a range of pink and apricot iris flowers which I managed to track down to a specialist nursery in Suffolk. It is rather a nice story. Sarah Cook was head gardener at Sissinghurst for 14 years. One day she found an iris 'Benton Nigel' growing in the borders there which sparked childhood memories of helping her mother do teas in the Suffolk village of Benton End where they sold iris seedlings. Now retired from Sissinghurst, Sarah has begun her own specialist collection of Benton irises from her home in Suffolk. Unlike most modern bearded irises, Cedric Morris colours are subtler, the flowers more elegant. He bred an enormous range including the first pink iris 'Edward of Windsor'. Sarah now has the national collection of Sir Cedric Morris irises. This summer my Benton irises flowered for the first time so I was able to paint them.

Mixed purple and blue tall bearded irises with Allium aflatunense *and* Tulipa *'Negrita' in a watercolour painting by Ann.*
20 × 28 INCHES

*The subtle colours of
Sir Cedric Morris irises
flowering in their first
year after planting in the
garden at Shepherd House
in 2012. Watercolour
painting by Ann.*

22 × 29 INCHES

Lord Warden

Edward of Windsor

Benton Buff

Benton Pewdie

Benton Graeme

Benton Susan

Ann Fraser 2012

Painting Hellebores

above *Watercolour painting by Ann of mixed hellebores from the garden at Shepherd House. Yellow hellebores are quite rare, this one was lent to Ann by Beryl McNaughton of Macplants.*
20 × 28 INCHES

below *A selection of mainly Ashwood garden hybrid hellebores growing in the garden.*

Hellebores are another favourite. The acid green flowers of *Helleborus argutifolius* brighten dull winter and spring days and their habit of seeding around and popping up where they know they will be happy is particularly appealing. The Lenten Rose or *Helleborus orientalis* is always engaging and the modern hybrids can be spectacular, ranging through whites, yellows, pinks, purples to dark slatey blacks – as well as the picotee flowers edged with contrasting colours. They all hide their real beauty by hanging their heads; lift their faces and you are amazed by their different shades, patterns and spots. We frequently place small mirrors under the drooping flower heads so that we can see their faces.

I cut all the old leaves off when the flower heads have appeared above the soil, usually in early January, and give them a feed of bone meal and maybe some compost. They resent being disturbed in the garden and they immediately wilt if picked so to paint them I either have to dig up a whole clump or buy new plants in flower – I usually opt for the latter! Ashwood Nurseries who have a wonderful selection of hellebores is a good stopping off point when we are on the way to visit our son in Herefordshire.

A wonderful slate blue, almost black, hellebore bred by Helen Ballard. Watercolour painting by Ann.
9 × 7 INCHES

Painting Poppies

above *Stunning red oriental poppies taken against dark background.*

above right *Red oriental poppies growing with Aquilegia canadensis.*

My fourth favourite has to be the poppy. The buds have a hairy casing, two lobes which part to show the brilliant crumpled petals resembling crushed silk. To make them last in water so that they can have their portrait painted, I burn the ends of their stems immediately after picking. The oriental poppies are the real showmen and although they have a short flowering season I would not be without them. There are so many new varieties like Patty's Plum that are worth seeking out. The opium poppy *Papaver somniferum* seeds itself with gay abandon and you never know what colour you will get. The jewels of the May garden are the blue Himalayan poppy *Meconopsis*, only rediscovered in 1924 by Kingdon Ward. They are difficult to grow in dry light soil as they prefer cool moist conditions. They are the most exquisite blue of the whole plant kingdom and must have caused quite a stir when first displayed at the Chelsea

opposite, clockwise from top *Three watercolours by Ann:*

Oriental poppy 'Patties Plum'
7 × 10 INCHES

Oriental poppy 'Coral Reef'
10 × 14 INCHES

Oriental poppy 'Perry's White'
10 × 14 INCHES

Meconopsis x sheldonii from the Chinese hillside Royal Botanic Garden Edinburgh   June 2000   Ann Fraser

Gentiana sino-ornata 'The Caley' Ann Fraser Oct 2009

Flower Show. During the time that I was a trustee of the RBGE, I was commissioned to paint *Meconopsis × sheldonii* for the retiring Chairman, Professor Malcolm Wilkins and was permitted to be able to pick some samples from the Botanics. (Again, they last for ages if you burn their stems immediately after picking.) What a magnificent plant, I only wish that we could grow them at Shepherd House.

Those are the four which I most enjoy painting and growing. There are of course many others not mentioned and not only flowers. I frequently paint fruit, vegetables, leaves, berries and mixtures of plants growing happily together as they do in the garden. Everything I paint we grow at Shepherd House. I enjoy putting plants together both in the garden and in my paintings, sometimes composing 'Dream Borders' which are flights of fancy in the sense that the flowers they portray do not grow in such close proximity to one another or even at the same time but are composed on the page to create a harmonious picture. I am lucky not to have to look far for inspiration; everything is there growing in the garden and if a flower dies I can readily pick another.

Garden or painting: which came first? I conclude that it is the passion for plants that combines them both.

*English Florist Tulip
'Akers Flame' painted by
Ann for an exhibition at
Yorkshire Sculpture Park
of English Florists' Tulips.*
12 × 9 INCHES

Aconitum vosene, Tall bearded Iris 'Scintillation', Papaver Black and White, Tulipa 'Maureen' and Queen of the Night', Aquilegia Magpie, Cistus × cyprius, Digitalis 'Alba', Rosa Nevada, Lilium martagon album, Papaver somniforum, Viola 'Molly Sanderson' July 2008

above 'Dream Border' a painting
by Ann featuring the nearly black
Iris 'Superstition', the tulip 'Queen of
the Night', white foxglove, Aquilegia
'Magpie', oriental poppy 'Black and
White', Lillium martagon album
and others.

20 × 28 INCHES

right Ann calls this painting black and
white spring: tulip 'Queen of the Night',
lily-flowered tulip 'White Triumphator',
summer snowflake Leucojium
aestivum, Fritillaria meleagris, Trillium
chloropetalum and snowdrops, all
growing in the wild garden.

20 × 14 INCHES

13 Butterflies

left *Ann likes to add butterflies to her paintings and usually adds one that she has seen in the garden at the time of the painting. Sadly a fritillary butterfly has never been seen in the garden but Ann liked the similarity of the chequered pattern on its wings to that of Fritillaria meleagris.*
20 × 14 INCHES

right *Butterflies from the collection in Canna House, painted while we were staying with John and Margaret Lorne Campbell.*
9 × 14 INCHES

[ANN] Butterflies have always fascinated me. As a small child in India I was given a butterfly net and many happy hours were spent in trying to catch the numerous exotic butterflies in our garden at Bally House, though probably without much success.

I frequently put butterflies in my paintings and try to include one that I have seen flying at the time I am painting a particular plant. Some years ago I sent away for a collection of butterflies and still use these today as reference.

Sadly I have definitely noticed that the number of butterflies in the garden has dwindled over the years. Like changing colours of the leaves, their arrival marks changing seasons. We usually get Orange Tips, Small Tortoiseshells and sometimes Peacocks in the spring, Whites in the summer and Red Admirals and Peacocks in the autumn.

We have two or three times seen hummingbird hawk moths in the

above *Cordoned crab apples 'Red Sentinel' create great interest in the garden from spring blossom right up to Christmas with their bright red fruits.*

courtyard garden hovering over the lavender. They behave just like the real humming birds that we have seen in Costa Rica.

We were very privileged to get to know John and Margaret Lorne Campbell of The Isle of Canna, one of the Small Isles in the Inner Hebrides. A renowned conservationist John netted his first butterfly at the age of 11 and was still adding to his collection 60 years later. His stunning collection is now to be preserved as a unique record of insect life on the west coast of Scotland. Once, when staying with them on Canna we had a very wet spell of weather and were not able to get out. I asked if I could paint some of his butterflies. He readily agreed and I have the painting to this day, a wonderful reminder of our most unusual and valued friends.

opposite *A commission for a good friend. We frequently see Red Admiral butterflies in the garden on a warm November day.* 20 × 14 INCHES

Malus 'Red Sentinel'   Ann Fraser November 2012

14 Livestock, Domestic & Otherwise

left Some of Charlie's white fantail pigeons taking a bath. The rill is a great attraction for all sorts of garden birds – and small children.

right Silkie bantams have full run of the garden in winter and spring.

[CHARLIE] The white fantail pigeons originally lived in the hayloft above the stable. When the stable was redeveloped as a cottage the pigeons were evicted and reluctantly removed to a custom-built dovecot loft above the garage. A sparrow hawk makes regular raids, but the pigeons, breeding energetically, seem to hold their own.

Hens, Muscovy ducks and a Chinese goose grazed the wilderness which is today our wild garden. Currently we have white silkie bantams and they have their own coop and run beside the four compost bins but later when seeds have germinated and grown to be hen scratch proof the silkies are allowed the whole run of the garden. If we forget to shut them up at night Mr Fox scales our 10 ft walls (how does he do it?) kills the hens and carries off his booty across the walls to wherever his den is located.

The exotic male of Lady Amherst's Pheasant. Sometimes seen in the wild, this pheasant prefers to run rather than fly. We had three in the garden for several years but sadly all were eaten by Mr Fox.

Being next door to Pinkiehill Farm, the odd rat has been known to take up residence in our large compost bins. They have proved much too clever for East Lothian's Rat Catchers (now of course called Pest Control Executives) and relish the poisons that are said to be painlessly lethal. Fed up by all this I became quite ruthless. I have caught a few in horrible traps, glove-handled, and I find that the rats soon come to realise that they are up against a determined enemy and they decamp to seek asylum in a less horrid owner's compost heap.

A tame cock pheasant sought sanctuary in our garden for ages. Golden pheasants and, recently, magnificent Lady Ameshurst pheasants have also graced our lawn but Mr Fox, denied access to our white silkies, found pheasant to be a tasty alternative and has alas scoffed the lot.

The larger of our two ponds is home to whopping carp and golden orfe. Herons spy them as they commute from sea to River Esk but herons like to wade and our pond being deep they would be out of their depth if they attempted to do so.

For years a pair of mallard duck arrived at the pond in April. The pair would each year become a lone drake until three weeks later a proud duck

above left

Robert aged 18 months feeding the golden pheasant that lived with us for many years.

Mallard duck with her ducklings. For years she came and hatched her brood (sometimes as many as 12) but we never discovered where she nested. When they became too big for the pond we had to summon our neighbours to help us escort mother and ducklings across the busy road to Inveresk Lodge so that they could get to the river.

with twelve or so ducklings would swim down the rill and live with us until sufficiently grown to face the dangers of life on the river.

There have been marked changes in our wild bird population. There are now few house sparrows where 50 years or so ago clouds of them would infuriate us by shredding newly germinated rows of lettuce. Ring doves were unknown; now the garden is home to a pair and several more feed beneath the bird table. Goldfinches were rarely seen and now are common.

We plant shrubs and trees for our pleasure but what has been created seems to please garden birds galore and nest boxes here and there are usually occupied by contented tenants.

above right

Golden Orfe have grown to quite a size and have bred in the pond. We feed them twice a day in summer but not at all in winter.

Our rough haired dachshund 'Katie': a constant companion in the garden.

15 Snowdrops

left *Galanthus 'Fred's Giant': Fred Sutherland, who found the original clump of this plant in the 1950s, was head gardener at Cruickshank Botanic Garden in Aberdeen. Fred's Giant has been treated somewhat dismissively by recent books on snowdrops but we find it a really good doer, increasing rapidly.*

right *Given to Ann by a school friend, Percy Picton has spread into large clumps in the garden and is now the most prolific and most loved of all our special snowdrops.*

[ANN] I think there are more poems written about snowdrops than any other flower. Coleridge, Tennyson and Wordsworth all wrote poems on snowdrops. I have printed some of them and when our garden is open for snowdrops I display the poems beside them. 'Ode to the Snowdrop' by Mary Robinson (1758–1800) is one of my favourites and extends to five verses. The first reads:

> *The snow-drop Winter's timid child,*
> *Awakes to life, bedew'd with tears,*
> *And flings around its fragrance mild;*
> *And where no rival flow'rets bloom,*
> *Amidst the bare and chilling gloom,*
> *A beauteous gem appears!*

Galanthus Elwesii
    'Mrs Macnamara'
An early flowering snowdrop,
collected in the Caucasus by
Mrs. Macnamara, Dylan Thomas's
mother-in-law   January 2008

Ann Fraser

Galanthus
plicatus
'Colossus'

Ann Fraser
January 2008

This is what Ann calls the 'Snowdrop Theatre', where we display some of the special snowdrops for garden openings.

Snowdrops help you through the winter. My first snowdrops flower at Christmas and I still have snowdrops flowering in March and April. Being a small garden we do not have acres of snowdrops as do many of the large houses in Scotland but we do have a growing collection of named cultivars and species. My interest in snowdrops began when a school friend of mine who has a well-known snowdrop garden asked me to do a painting of some of her special snowdrops. As I only had the common snowdrops at the time (brought from my parent's house at Sunlaws) she sent me her selection of five different cultivars and said I would be welcome to plant them in the garden when the painting was finished. This I did and promptly forgot all about them or where I had planted them until they reappeared the following spring. Some years later with the help of Beryl McNaughton of Macplants, an expert on snowdrops, I was able to identify them. This really started my interest in collecting.

On many visits to the RHS London show in February I have bought more cultivars to add to the collection and have become completely hooked. I now grow about 70 different cultivars and species and open the garden in February for The Scottish Snowdrop Festival. Not only do I display poems beside the snowdrops but also some of the stories about them which are fascinating. We very often have more visitors for our open day in February than we have later in the year.

As Charlie says, at first sight snowdrops all look the same but after a time you begin to recognise the differences. The time of flowering, the size, shape and colour of the leaves, then the size, shape and markings on the flowers – it quickly becomes addictive. Although the special ones are very expensive to buy, in a few years they bulk up and can be divided and given to friends, sold or just spread around the garden. Some of my favourites that do especially well in this garden are Percy Picton, Colossus, Lady Ephinstone, Mrs Macnamara, Fred's Giant, Armine and Little Ben. All have stories to tell.

Watercolour painting of Galanthus 'Percy Picton' by Ann. A beautiful tall snowdrop with large flowers hanging from a long pedicel, sometimes produces two flowers simultaneously, enhancing the impact of this graceful snowdrop. It increases freely into large floriferous clumps.

12 × 9 INCHES

Galanthus plicatus
'Percy Picton'
A very fine snowdrop, originating
from the garden of the late
Percy Picton of Old Court Nursery
Worcestershire in the early 1870s
Ann Fraser February 2008

16 Topiary

[CHARLIE] It all started with a large and rather sad looking box bush near to our kitchen window.

It was there when we purchased the house, lonely and shapeless and surrounded by bishop's weed. In its shapelessness I thought I could see a broody hen and that is what it became at least to my eye, though rarely to that of our visitors. The bishop's weed gone, I planted a small box egg to complete the image. The broody hen, looked less and less like the real thing as years passed so I wrung its neck. It has gone but the egg remains as a reminder of my first attempts at topiary.

We have always had dachshunds and two box ones now guard our back door looking rather more ferocious than Katie our present incumbent. She enjoys our garden visitors and is much more welcoming than her remote, smooth haired cousins that belonged to a late and important garden owner in Sussex.

In 1999, I clipped what I thought was a beautiful butterfly out of an overgrown shrubby lonicera bush. A guest arriving just prior to the Millennium said 'I see you have captured the Millenium Bug'. When that non event had passed without the anticipated disasters, I executed my equally disastrous butterfly.

Patience and time are required with box clipping – *Buxus sempervirens* is never speedy virens! It takes about a week to clip the box in the main garden and another week to do the front but my week is not five days 9 till 5, rather it is a week when I feel like tackling it and if I get bored I turn to another garden task. I do it all by hand. My thirty-two cones, pyramids and balls in the potager are evidence of patience if not artistic merit and they are an important feature of the garden as well as providing much needed structure in the winter.

I claim no great skill in topiary, but it is fun and a selection of my efforts line the yew hedge: a cock, a hen, a pheasant, a rabbit, the beginnings of a Grecian urn and a selection of indefinable shapes which perhaps add something to the garden, though I'm not quite sure what.

The neatly clipped box of what we call the Herb Parterre. Box squares are filled with cotton lavender (Santolina chamaecyparissus), common rue (Ruta graveolens) and lavender.

above *The original large broody hen which lived with us for many years before its neck was cruelly wrung! Pink tulips in the herb parterre.*
PHOTO: VIVIAN RUSSELL

opposite above *One of the very productive pear arbours enhanced by cones of neatly clipped box.*

opposite below *The old potting shed with some of Charlie's topiary.*

top *Looking across the courtyard garden towards the terrace.*

above *The courtyard garden later in the year. Clipped box and holly adds interest throughout the year and especially in winter.*

right *Looking towards the cottage, the courtyard garden in 2010 at tulip time; again topiary punctuates the view.*

Shepherd House dates from 1690 and has been the home of Charles and Ann Fraser since 1957. It is situated in the village of Inveresk where there have been settlements since Roman Times. The curved gables suggest Dutch influence.

17 Garden Open Today

left *Painting by Ann from 1995, inspired by the wonderful ancient illuminated manuscripts.*
27 × 20 INCHES

right *Teas are served in the conservatory at garden openings. Homemade cakes, drop scones and cookies all made by Ann are always much enjoyed. We have a loyal group of wonderful helpers but none in their first flush of youth (including Ann!) so we have decided only to do teas for the village garden openings and visiting groups.*

[ANN] The larger gardens in the village of Inveresk have been opening under Scotland's Gardens Scheme since after the war. In 1964 when the children were young we thought it would be a good idea to have a family friendly fete in aid of children's charities in our garden on the same day that the village gardens were open.

We encouraged the children to run stalls, side shows and raffles and the older children to organise a 'creche' where parents could leave their children whilst going round the gardens. This was all a great success and got the whole village involved. The Children's Fete continued every year that the Inveresk gardens were open until 1978 when it was felt that our garden was of a standard to join in with the village gardens open day.

Opening the garden for the first time is always slightly daunting, but opening under the village banner made it much easier. In these days there were seven or eight gardens wanting to open, and for a time we split it into large gardens on one day and smaller gardens on another. Gradually over the years the owners wanting to open their gardens dwindled and in 1993 we took the plunge and opened on our own.

We are fortunate to be an entirely walled garden. Not only do the walls provide shelter but they create a certain mystery to the garden visitor as to what lies behind. In 1991 *American House and Garden* magazine sent Rosemary Verey to write an article on the garden. As I have mentioned before I was a great fan of hers and wondered how she would react to all the ideas that we had pinched from her garden at Barnsley. However I needn't have worried as having taken her round she gave me a great hug and wrote a stunning article. This launched us on to the garden magazine trail. Since then we have had articles in many glossy magazines and our garden visitors have multiplied. We have also appeared in *The Beechgrove Garden* which all helps to encourage visitors.

Opening under Scotland's Gardens Scheme you are permitted to give 40% of the gross takings from garden openings to your own choice of charity. The remainder goes to Scotland's Gardens Scheme beneficiaries and over the years we must have given over £50,000 to charity which makes it all worthwhile.

Garden visitors are very appreciative and Charlie and I enjoy meeting them. We have decided that there are two types of visitors: those that 'see' and say what a lovely garden after a ten minute tour and those that 'look', remark on every plant, have a notebook, don't miss a thing and stay in the garden for an hour or more. Visitors who constantly refer to their own garden make me wonder why they bothered to come, and those who bombard you with compliments, whilst very satisfactory can be a bit overwhelming. We enjoy hearing other people's ideas and criticisms and are sometimes triggered by visitors' suggestions to take the idea further. We have had visiting groups from all over the world, some from cruise ships. In 2011 we even had a group from Russia from The Moscow School of Design.

[CHARLIE] When we held our first children's fete each child had to choose and manage their own event. Someone had donated a Hornby train set with rails, tunnels and stations and we decided that should be raffled. Simon our eldest son, then aged five, saw the train set and said, 'I want that'. It was explained what a raffle was and a few tickets were bought for him. He stood throughout the afternoon staring at the train set and as if by magic had the winning ticket. That took a bit more explaining.

Our children's fete made the princely sum of £40 for the Children's League of which 10% went to Scotland's Gardens Scheme, thus our first

donation to the Scheme was £4 for which we received a glowing letter of thanks.

Since then the sum has grown over the years to a substantial amount of more than £50,000 as Ann has mentioned. The charities benefiting from our garden openings are now too numerous to list but include The Princess Royal's Trust for Carers, The Princes Trust, Paintings in Hospital, The Musselburgh War Memorial, Music in Hospitals, The Art Fund, The Prestonpans Tapestry Appeal and Help for Heroes.

In addition we have on several occasions held evening parties to support various organisations and these have included the John Muir Trust, Patrons of the National Galleries of Scotland, Gardening Leave and Lamp of the Lothians. Proceeds from our many visiting groups add to the sums donated.

We garden because we enjoy it but it adds to our pleasure that other people enjoy visiting us and an additional satisfaction is the support we have been able to give to the organisations above.

Raising money for Music in Hospitals at a garden opening, our visitors enjoy a duet in the May sunshine.

19 Garden Visiting

left *The pale colour of tall bearded iris 'Jane Philips' blends with the soft pink of oriental poppy 'Cedric Morris' in the courtyard garden.*

right *A Finlay-ism? Old watering can in 'Shepherd House Blue' with* Myosotis arvensis *(forget-me-not) painted on it, an idea inspired by Ian Hamilton Finlay.*

[ANN] We end our garden openings at the beginning of July, and take a week off to visit other gardens. Over many years, we have been as far as India, Spain, Italy and France to look at gardens but more often we explore different areas of the UK.

In Scotland we are lucky enough to have two iconic, unique gardens. Little Sparta, created by the late Ian Hamilton Finlay, and Portrack House (Garden of Cosmic Speculation) designed by Charles Jencks.

Far from being unique, our garden is an amalgam of other people's ideas. As Charlie says, there is no copyright in garden design and many of our ideas have been inspired by visits to other gardens. The skill is to adapt an idea to fit your own space, sometimes it is only a plant association and sometimes a major alteration.

Gardens that have inspired us over the years are Barnsley House for its

The cordoned crab apples 'Red Sentinel' in full blossom, making a delicate division between the courtyard garden and lawn.

potager, Tyninghame Walled Garden for the Nepeta Walk, Hestercombe Gardens and Generalife, at the Alhambra, for the rills, Crathes Castle Garden for the yew hedges and enclosed rooms, Royal Botanic Garden Edinburgh for the alpine wall, Alnwick (top garden) for the cordoned crab apples, Highgrove for the bulb meadow, Little Sparta for the garden sentences, Newby Hall for their collection of *Cornus*, Helen Dillon's garden for her colour coordination and Roy Strong's garden at The Laskett for a sense of drama.

Maybe in turn our garden visitors find something at Shepherd House that can be adapted and translated to small plots anywhere.

[CHARLIE] A sense of excitement comes over me when I go through yet another garden gate. What will I find? I nearly always do find something that I can relate to. In Snowshill Manor in Gloucestershire I found this verse:

> *Hours fly, flowers die,*
> *New days, new ways,*
> *Pass by.*
> *Love stays.*

I am often asked which is my favourite garden and I answer, 'The one I visit next', though I do have a weakness for quirky gardens. One of my favourites is Herterton House in Northumberland. It is about the size of our garden and Frank and Marjorie Lawley who have created it are a delightful couple, always welcoming and keen to share their knowledge of gardening. The garden is cleverly divided into garden rooms each with a theme. There is no lawn. Frank has done all the hard landscaping himself, including building a two-storey gazebo. He is clearly an expert. I'm

Rosemary Verey visiting the garden in 1991 to write an article for American House and Garden.

not! They have a tremendous knowledge and love of plants. You leave Herterton with one of Marjorie's special plants, dug up from the nursery by the owner herself, and a song in your heart, newly aware that gardens, wonderful as they are, are made by people. The one needs the other. A garden lived in by those who created it is of much more interest than an institutionalised one, frozen in time.

Likewise I enjoy our own visitors. Musicians need an audience and so do gardens. It delights me to share ours and I learn from conversing with the visitors. There are a few regular conversations: 'What a lot of work!' slightly grates and is now met by, 'On the contrary what a lot of pleasure'.

We began by opening one day in the year. This has grown to two or three such days including, as Ann's collection of snowdrops grew, one in February when Ann's soup takes over from her home baking. We also open on Tuesday and Thursday afternoons, with an honesty box, from April till July.

We have experienced little theft although a prized *Trillium* disappeared and on another occasion whilst I was talking to someone, a visitor interrupted to ask if she could take a seedpod from an oriental poppy and without thinking I replied, 'Of course'. Then I realised that the poppy had not flowered, what could she be talking about? Rushing across the garden I found the culprit had gone but before doing so had snipped off not the seedpod, for there were none but all the buds of a favourite poppy that was about to flower.

That was not an interesting visitor but most are. Recently I was chatting up a pretty girl and after a pleasant conversation of 'Where do you live?' and 'Are you a gardener?' I came into the kitchen where a group of wonderful ladies helping with the teas were all of a flutter. 'Do you know who you were speaking to?' I, of course, hadn't the slightest idea. It seems my pretty girl was Nicole Kidman. The ladies were unimpressed that I had never heard of her and irritated further by my question, 'Was she the pretty one in *The Sound of Music*?' So I hurried out at their command to learn more about our famous visitor. En route I met a retired professor of physics at Edinburgh University who had helped in the search for the Higgs Boson. That was interesting and meantime, to the disgust of the tea ladies, my new friend Nicole had gone.

One other visitor who came to see the snowdrops no doubt spied the carefully labelled groups but said she wanted to admire swathes of snowdrops like Dalmeny. Well, our one acre garden is not Dalmeny. The visitor asked for her money back, this we happily agreed to. It is perhaps because the garden is just one acre and not vast like many of the great gardens, that visitors can relate to Shepherd House. It seems to delight the visitor as it does Ann and me.

clockwise from top left

Pink buds of Rhododendron *'Loderi King George' open to large sweetly smelling trusses of pale pink flowers.*

Deep red flowers over mottled green and brown foliage of the strong growing Trillium kurabayashi.

Helleborus × ballardiae *'Pink Frost' a very floriferous plant starts flowering before the end of the year.*

One of Sir Cedric Morris Irises 'Benton Deirdre'.

19 Garden Style
& Plant Association

left Geranium *'Orian'*, Lupin *'Masterpiece'* and the later flowering Allium *'Ambassador'* make a very satisfactory cool combination.

right *In winter, red crab apples contrast with the blue of the posts. The crab apples stay on the plants until well into the New Year when they are devoured by hungry blackbirds.*

[ANN] I am not sure what the difference is between design and style but I think that design is the basic planning of the garden and style is what you put in it.

Our own style of garden is very much dictated by the high stone walls which form an equilateral triangle in the middle of the village (we are really just a triangular traffic island behind walls!). Garden visitors sometimes say the garden is 'paradise' and of course the literal meaning of this old Persian word is 'walled enclosure'.

Our first attempt at design, as has been mentioned previously, was to restore the central path shown on eighteenth century maps. To extend the vista we built the formal pond and then the steps down to the old fashioned garden so that we would have a vista from the house right to the back wall of the garden. This gave us a formal framework from which

Crown imperial Fritillaria imperialis *'Lutea' against a background of golden* Philadelphus.

Tulip 'Mickey Mouse' growing beside Euphorbia palustris.

The lily-flowered tulip 'Ballerina' is an absolute must in the hot border. The vivid orange flowers which are also scented always catch the eye.

to work. Gertrude Jekyll's gardening style was to have formality near the house and more natural gardening further away which seems to fit perfectly (quite by accident) into what we have created at Shepherd House.

In 1994 Rosemary Verey asked us if we would write about our own garden in a forthcoming book on *Secret Gardens, Revealed by Their Owners*. As we both had very different ideas we asked Rosemary if we could each write 500 words to which she readily agreed.

I loved Frances Hodgson Burnett's novel as a child. I loved the idea of a secret garden. I began writing the article with a quotation taken from the book which at the time rather summed up our style of gardening. 'Where you tend a rose, a thistle cannot grow.' Sadly, planting intensively does not mean that weeds cannot grow but it certainly helps and

A dark hellebore flowering beside Erythronium *'Pagoda', an excellent doer in this garden.*

above, left to right

Contrasting late flowering single tulips 'Maureen' and 'Havran'.

Tulips 'Raspberry Ripple' and 'Bleu Amiable' match perfectly when grown together.

Double late flowering tulip 'Carnival de Nice' (this a very long lived tulip in our garden) growing amongst the dark cow parsley 'Ravenswing'.

we have always planted intensively. It has its drawbacks as we discovered 10 years later when we found we had a very shady garden. However there are many similarities at Shepherd House Garden to the magical garden Mary Lennox entered: the high stone walls, the single entrance door, the winding paths, the roses climbing up the old apple trees and the curtains of ivy hanging over the walls. Many visitors comment that it is indeed a secret garden as there is no clue outside the walls as to what lies inside. Judging by the numbers of visitors it is no longer a secret.

In Rosemary Verey's book we came under the heading of 'Exuberant Gardens'. I am certainly keen on exuberant plants as they are the ones I love to paint; the tulips, oriental poppies and irises I have mentioned.

Species tulip Tulipa batalini *'Bright Gem' flowering in amongst* Euphorbia myrsinites *on the alpine wall. All the species tulips come up every year.*

We also have many roses not only in the rose border but climbing over pergolas and arches and up trees. Height in a garden is invaluable.

Another important aspect of a garden is scent. I love going out into the garden on a warm summer's evening when you really notice the scent. Winter perfume is just as important and I have placed *Sarcococca*, the

left *Colour contrasts: Iris 'Quechee' in front of the blue seat with oriental poppy 'Beauty of Livermere' behind.*

above left *Tall bearded iris 'Jane Philips' growing with* Geranium *'Brookside' in the courtyard garden.*

above right *Mixed tall bearded irises growing against the cottage wall.*

Not so secret: entrance to Shepherd House Garden.

A Haddonstone urn in the far corner of the garden planted with white Argyranthemum, violas, *and petunias. To the right is* Cornus kousa *(flowering dogwood) which regularly flowers for us in late May.*

Looking through the blue gate to the compost heap.

winter box, beside the garden path so even in winter you have wonderful wafts of scent whenever you walk past.

When we first planned the borders we went for the mixed style of planting incorporating trees, shrubs, perennials and bulbs in the same border. In a small garden this is quite a good idea as it means that there is something of interest all the year round and it also adds structure in the winter. Herbaceous borders are wonderful if you have a lot of space but they lack structure in the winter. I have already touched on colour schemes but evidently one does have a favourite colour and looking

Our Wisteria *took fifteen years to flower and then it wasn't the good blue that we expected. However we have grown to enjoy its rather dusky pinkish flowers.*

White wisteria (Wisteria floribunda album) *clothes the blue arch in late May.*

Rosa 'Ghislaine de Feligonde' covers one of the blue pillars in front of the cascading pink clusters of Rosa 'Mme d'Arblay' *which used to climb up the blue cedar, now deceased.*

Tall bearded iris 'Jane Philips' growing in front of Rosa banksiae 'Lutea' *which climbs the steps to the old pigeon loft. This rose, we were told, is not hardy in Scotland but it thrives in this sheltered corner.*

round our garden I realise that we have many more blue and purple plants than any other. I am not frightened of using very bright colours but tend to group them in one area of the garden softened by grasses. Grouping plants together in the garden is similar to composing a painting but on paper at least you know that they will not seed around thus spoiling your colour composition.

I have no idea what our style of gardening is but we garden primarily for ourselves and it is the style that pleases us. If gardening didn't give you pleasure and satisfaction you wouldn't do it.

A well-trained Pyracantha *at the garden entrance.*

20 Guerrilla Gardening

left *Cornflowers and corn marigolds mark the front entrance to Shepherd House, one of my favourite colour combinations.*

right Lavandula angustifolia *'Hidcote' grows on the roadside outside the cottage we let for holidays.*

[CHARLIE] The high walls round the garden deny me the opportunity of adding more acres. Dreams of a tunnel under the main road into the National Trust for Scotland's garden at Inveresk Lodge and down to the river are, I guess, unrealistic. But in a small way we have gardened beyond our walls. We started by planting unwanted irises outside the whole length of the west wall. Although initially this was a success, over the years weeds have infiltrated. Some irises still flourish. Others have died and the strip is now colonised by valerian, some white but mostly red and by *Euphorbia characias*. East Lothian Council who maintain the grass there have left the newcomers and I guess I will too.

At the front gates, outside the wall we have two very dry beds in which I plant tulips and wallflower every year, followed by bright coloured annuals to enliven the entry to our front garden.

To the left of the garden entrance, the garage garden in full bloom with tulips. Between two tiered yews, we have placed a seat for the weary to rest.

[ANN] The idea of planting at the front gate was inspired by a visit to Arabella Lennox Boyd's garden near Lancaster. We were with our very good American friends Mel and Janine Luke who had heard Arabella lecture in New York. Having done the research as to the whereabouts of the garden we got completely lost and after making several wrong turns we came across gates planted with yellow daisies and blue cornflower (one of my favourite colour combinations). We immediately knew that we were on the right track.

[CHARLIE] The east wall, again on the outside has been more successful than the west. Here we have planted *Alchemilla mollis* thus banishing this wonderful but over-prolific plant from the main garden where it would soon take over if left to fulfil its own seeding ambitions. Behind the *Alchemilla* I have planted the sedge *Carex elata* 'aurea', Bowles Golden Sedge, a pairing I discovered on one of our garden visiting trips, which puts on a good show annually.

The stable, hayloft and shed were converted into a cottage in 1973, designed by our excellent architect Ian Begg. Now we let the cottage by the week through Scottish Country Cottages. Outside the cottage two tiny lawns are edged by a lavender hedge. That has worked well although I find that it puts on an excellent show for 10 to 12 years before it eventually gets a bit woody and requires replacing.

There was originally no access to the back garden other than through the house or the garages and neither was entirely suitable for barrowing dung or for our growing number of visitors. Ian Begg having retired, his partner Raymond Muszynski was now our architect and having successfully redesigned a farm cottage opposite our garages for us, he was commissioned to seek the necessary planning permission for a new entrance, the walls being listed. He designed a distinguished entry with an elegant wooden door to suit the period of the house in which he incorporated an ancient lock we had found in the garden in 1957. Above the new door we recently commissioned Gardner Molloy to engrave the words Shepherd House Garden. On the wall to the right of the gate we have trained *Pyracantha* along five horizontal wires, an idea we admired when visiting a Gloucestershire garden.

In front of the new door there is a cobbled area and on either side of the door two ancient chimney pots planted annually with trailing yellow begonias the colour of traffic warden's coats. Ann thinks these are plebeian (though she would never use that particular word). Beyond that, an area outside the wall was a spectacular wilderness of nettles, bishop's weed, brambles and a monstrous buddleia. I dug and weeded and bonfired until the area was clear. There are now no perennial weeds, indeed there are none in our whole garden as they are readily eradicated from the light, deep soil. Annual weeds however are still a challenge, the worst being 'sticky willie'. Ann designed a lay out for this area and into it we put unwanted plants and shrubs – those in excess of our garden needs or ones that have been tried and found wanting. All seem grateful to be given a second chance.

Between two tiered yews we have placed a seat against the wall to encourage passers-by to rest. Behind that, having willow wands left over from building our raised beds, I stuck them in as a screen and they too, pleased not to have been bonfired, have done their best for me.

Sadly, there are now no more areas to guerrilla garden; what a pity.

On the outside of our wall along the roadside we have planted Alchemilla mollis *and* Carex elata 'Aurea'.

21 The Gardening Year

[ANN] The gardening year for me begins and ends in November. This is when everything in the garden has died down and the clear-up begins which usually takes a couple of months. Yet the thrill of finding snowdrops and other spring bulbs pushing through the ground reminds you that the whole cycle is beginning again. This is also when I plant most of the tulips and since I regularly order over 1000 bulbs it takes quite a while. We have an excellent bulb planter (never buy a cheap one) which makes the job very easy even in the beds.

We don't usually get a lot of snow and when it comes it doesn't lie for long (except for the harsh winters of 2009/10 and 2010/11). The garden becomes a winter wonderland in the snow. Settling on all the shapes and structure it gives the garden an extra dimension, making the box parterres into magical patterns. I love it as long as it doesn't stay too long.

The slow progress of the seasons gives us time to forget and what happened last year becomes a distant memory. The succession of new delights encourages us to look forward and never back. A garden is never finished; it is constantly changing and maturing and never looks the same two years running. At this stage I have probably already planned which plants and shrubs I would like to cut back, move or take out. Herbaceous plants constantly need dividing, roses need pruning, young plants grown the previous year from seed, as well as last year's cuttings, all need new homes.

Moving plants around is what I call 'musical plants' and probably goes on till the end of March when the whole garden is mulched and fertilised. Gardening is a continuous creative adventure. During the winter months catalogues are read, previous notes consulted, seeds and new plants ordered and new schemes planned.

Our garden is best in the early months of the year. The stars of the show are snowdrops in February, hellebores in March, crocus, narcissus and fritillaries in April, tulips in May, irises and oriental poppies in June and roses in July. In July and August, apart from deadheading and generally tidying up we let the garden look after itself, and very often go on holiday.

Until 2011 we had a cottage at Boat of Garten beside the Spey, where we spent the whole month of August. My time was more often taken up with having family and friends to stay, and painting, so Charlie did the garden single handed although latterly we did have someone to cut the grass. By the time we returned home in September the garden at Shepherd House would be looking distinctly blowsy.

September and October can be magical with autumn colours but it is not long once again before we clear up ready for the winter. The fact that there is always in every month of the year something to look forward to is a boon in itself and the garden seldom lets you down.

In 1992 I decided to create a series of 12 paintings, one for each month of the year, depicting some of the plants growing in the garden. Each painting took me a month to paint and the series was awarded a Silver Gilt Medal when it was exhibited at the RHS Vincent Square London Show. I was short of material for the December painting and out for lunch one day spied a wonderful russet coloured mature medlar tree in our host's garden. I asked if I could take a small branch which was willingly granted. Charlie always says that we then had to buy a medlar to make an honest woman of me as everything else in the series was growing in the garden at Shepherd House. Our medlar is now 20 years old.

clockwise from top left: four seasons of colour

Under a snowy blanket Crab apple 'Red Sentinel'.

Ashwood Garden hybrid double hellebore.

Rose 'Ghislaine de Feligonde'.

Crab apple 'Golden Hornet'.

overleaf *A series of twelve paintings, one for each month of the year, depicting some of the plants growing in the garden. They were awarded a Silver Gilt Medal when exhibited in 1993 at the RHS Vincent Square, London Show.* EACH 20 × 28 INCHES

JANUARY

FEBRUARY

MAY

JUNE

SEPTEMBER

OCTOBER

MARCH

APRIL

JULY

AUGUST

NOVEMBER

DECEMBER

22 Taking Stock

[CHARLIE] Shepherd House and Inveresk have been central to the lives of the Fraser family for 55 years. We have had the good fortune to have wonderful neighbours, George and Jane Burnet of Rose Court who have lived in the village for longer than us. The village is indebted to them in countless ways. Two come immediately to mind. They formed the Inveresk Preservation Society which did so much in the early years to protect the village from the ravishes of ill conceived planning, and Jane's book *A Reason for Inveresk* educated us all about the history of the village and will encourage those that come after us to cherish what George and Jane have fought for. Harry and Marianne More Gordon of the Manor House are both artists and valued friends. Marianne is also the instigator and designer of Silver Jubilee and Diamond Jubilee quilts or hangings lovingly made by teams of locals to celebrate the Queen's extraordinary service to our country.

Dierama pulcherrimum
(*Angel's Fishing Rods*)
*are one of the main
features in the July garden
when many of the early
perennials are over. They
love the dry hot conditions
in the alpine wall and seed
themselves around with
gay abandon.*
PHOTO: VIVIAN RUSSELL

No designers were involved in the planning of our garden but experts have made helpful comments. As has been said we have planted and are still planting too many trees. Some years back we thought we must do something about this. George Anderson, then of the Royal Botanic Garden Edinburgh and latterly an outstanding president of the Royal Caledonian Horticultural Society, frequently brought students from the RBGE to our garden. He kindly volunteered to walk round the garden with us to give advice as to which trees, in his opinion, should be kept and which should go. This gave us confidence to remove a selection.

Several years later Sir Roy Strong who has built such a superb garden at The Laskett in Herefordshire, came to stay. He was giving a lecture for Scotland's Gardens Scheme on how he had renovated his garden and later walked round our garden and pointing to tree after tree said, 'Oh dear, that's got to go'. We did as he suggested and took down in total 12 trees. How right he was; more light, more space, new areas to plant new plants and even new trees but now we are more experienced in choosing the right tree for its space.

In our cottage opposite the garden entrance lived Jim Cox and his wife for 25 years. Jim was not a gardener but a good grass cutter until age made me wonder if I should be cutting his grass.

Pauline Mitchell has gardened for most of her life but as a mature student decided to take an MA at Edinburgh University. That achieved, a variety of career opportunities seemed possible but she now lives in our cottage and does a number of hours in our garden each week. When we are away she shows groups round the garden and looks after the place and our rough haired dachshund with love. Surprisingly she has an aversion to our lovely white silkie bantams.

I too have an aversion, to those of the horticultural school that believe gardens can be conserved because of the fame of some owner or designer. Gardens are living things and can no more be conserved than their owners can. So it is with Shepherd House. Change is part of the joy of gardening be it by the hour, the day or the year and we have new ideas each year.

Shepherd House is very special to the Frasers and is an important bond between Ann and me. She, the artist, has an eye for shape and colour that

The pond in early May with white 'Triumphator' tulips showing up against the coppery winter foliage of the beech pillars.

is absent in me, and her knowledge of plants is now profound. I like to get things done. Ann likes to get things right. We're a good team.

I have recently read *A Time to Plant*, the story of Hugh and Grania Cavendish's gardening life at Holker. It is ridiculous to compare Holker with its forty acres and Shepherd House with its one acre, but the Cavendishs and Frasers have something in common in their love of and commitment to their gardens. When a really good read ends and the book is finished there is a sense of loss. Happily, unlike a book, a garden is never finished. Early in our gardening careers we read that 'the process is the purpose'; this has been our gardening mantra ever since.

Ann and I will hope to have many more years of love and commitment to the garden and it is perhaps a compliment to our efforts that so many people enjoy visiting it. Kenneth Cox in his seminal book *Scotland for Gardeners* says in his entry for Shepherd House that it is an 'exquisite gem' and at the back of the book he lists Shepherd House as one of the great smaller gardens.

[ANN] Many articles in glossy magazines have been written about our garden and I hope it doesn't seem too boastful if we end our book with a selection of 'garden cuttings' – what other people have said about our garden. But before we get there I will choose just one perceptive quote. In 1992 Rosemary Verey wrote: 'The garden at Shepherd House reveals itself slowly, as a well-planned garden should ...' and she concludes, 'What began as an absorbing hobby is turning out to be a collaborative living work of art'.

It has certainly been a collaborative work. In 2012, Charlie, at the age of 84, finally retired from all his directorships and now spends all his waking hours either on the golf course or in the garden, frequently not coming in till after dark. I still love to get out there usually working two or three mornings every week. But a lot of my time is spent walking round the garden in all weathers just to enjoy it, to see what is flowering and to identify areas that need attention. We are now so fortunate to have Pauline who has taken over a lot of the jobs that I used to do. So now I am able to spend more time on painting and other commitments without feeling guilty that I should be working in the garden.

The garden has become such an important part of our lives and has grown and changed alongside the growing-up of children and now grandchildren. The garden is filled with memories of people as well as plants. To this day we remember who gave us which plant, instantly reminding us of that person who may no longer be with us. Charlie and I mostly agree about the important aspects of the garden but sometimes disagree about the method. Pruning comes to mind; he is inclined to be more severe than I would wish. 'Always prune in a rage', is his motto.

When we are gone I hope that some other gardener will get as much fun and satisfaction from the garden as we do. We do not garden for posterity, we garden for ourselves and we hope that those who come after us will do their own creative thing. It has been a shared journey, a combined passion and, together with the family, central to our long happy marriage.

23 Garden cuttings: what others say

[FAY YOUNG] Where to start? To be honest I did not fully realise what I was taking on when I suggested the editor should choose a selection of extracts from magazine and newspaper articles inspired by Shepherd House. In front of me is a daunting array of reviews stretching back over 20 years, a long line of writers describing the garden in all seasons and many weathers and quite a few of them making more than one visit.

Different garden writers come looking for different things but recurring themes emerge: the secret garden, the artist's garden, the evolving garden that never stands still – and the essential creative tension between contrasting and sometimes conflicting aims of the two people who have made the garden.

Of course there is an obvious place to start. The author and designer Rosemary Verey, described after her death in 2001 as the 'grande dame of English gardening writers,' opened the garden gate to a wider world in 1992 when her first article about Shepherd House was published in the American magazine *House & Garden*.

'The garden reveals itself slowly as a good garden should. There is no abrupt change,' she wrote after exploring every nook and cranny in the company of Ann, taking the path many other writers would follow, lingering enthusiastically over every border. 'A romantic gathering of colours, scent and historical association – how else can a rose garden create its magic?' And then pausing prophetically beneath tall trees at the end of the garden to ask herself, 'when will the cedar take over, I wonder'.

The piece also appeared in the UK *House & Garden* in 1994. That same year Mrs Verey invited Ann and Charlie to write about Shepherd House for her book *Secret Gardens: Revealed by Their Owners*.

'A secret garden?' asked Sean Hignett in *Scotland on Sunday* in 1994. 'The single acre of Shepherd House is in fact many secret gardens nestling into each other like a set of Chinese boxes.' From then on, Shepherd House has featured several times a year in a succession of glossy magazines, broadsheets, tabloids, weekend supplements and garden guides of all kinds – and in more than one language. 'Le Jardin d'une Artiste' was the focus of *Mon Jardin Ma Maison* in August 1997.

'The single acre of Shepherd House is in fact many secret gardens nestling into each other like a set of Chinese boxes.'
PHOTO: SHEILA SIM

Suki Urquhart, writing for *Caledonia* in 1999, notes the clever use of vistas and formal layouts to create the 'impression of pleasing symmetry' in an irregular triangle. She also observes the human elements. 'In Rosemary Verey's book *Secret Gardens* Charles Fraser acknowledges his wife's contribution as an eye for design and a knowledge of plants and modestly wonders what his own is. Having visited Shepherd House I can tell you … his contribution is crucial. In just an acre of ground so much is crammed into various different small garden rooms that if it were not kept tidy the design would be blurred. Charles weeds, clips, cuts, tidies, cultivates the ornamental potagers and makes compost …'

The following year Suki was back again to write for the *Sunday Times* about Ann's skill in growing plants for painting, 'in a series of discreet spaces linked by a sun-dappled arched walk festooned with old fashioned roses'.

Ann's 'marriage of art and science' was the special focus of Iain Gale's article for *Country Life* in 2006. In *Artist with Green Fingers* he looks closely at the work of 'one of the country's most sought after and acclaimed botanical painters' finding: 'details drawn in, not with the precision of an architect, but with just enough sufficient attention to be utterly convincing'. And behind that: 'dialogues with and about nature … a fascination with the way in which plants interrelate in the bigger picture'.

It is easy to forget Shepherd House garden is confined to one acre. Many reviews comment on the deceptively small scale – 'a single acre, a small wonder' – and perhaps that makes it all the more remarkable how often Shepherd House is listed as a 'must-see' in company with very much larger gardens. In March 2002, reviewing Scotland's Garden Scheme brochure, the *Daily Telegraph* picked Shepherd House as one of the most interesting gardens – along with Floors Castle, Crathes, Pitmedden, Dunrobin, Edzell and Leith Hall.

Again, in 2007 the *Telegraph* identifies Shepherd House as one of '50 best gardens to visit this summer' – some of the others included Kew Botanic Gardens and the private gardens of three of Britain's most celebrated gardeners, Beth Chatto, Helen Dillon and Christopher Lloyd.

Surprise and change are common themes in the press cuttings. 'Nothing stands still in this vibrant garden,' observes Julia Watson in *The English Garden* in March 2003, 'Gradual evolution … has produced an elegant formal garden with lots of surprises'. In 2004, writing for *The Times*, Vanessa Berridge detects: 'Behind the formality a whiff of Romance'. In 2007 on one of her many visits to the garden Antoinette Galbraith describes 'A fabulous formal garden full of spring colour'.

By 2009 Shepherd House is selected as one of Scotland's Top Ten Gardens by Ken Cox and Julie Edmonstone in the *Scottish Field*, because of

'a meld of clever design and excellent choice and cultivation of plants'. This time the other gardens included some of the most spectacular and flamboyant: Ian Hamilton Finlay's Little Sparta, Charles Jenck's Garden of Cosmic Speculation and the Royal Botanic Garden Edinburgh.

And so it continues; the garden growing, developing and constantly stimulating new interest and articles, right up to the present. In the early spring of 2012 Antoinette Galbraith came to see the snowdrops and, writing for *Scotland on Sunday*, finds the essence of Shepherd House: 'A strong characteristic of this garden is the way it keeps reinventing itself, changing with the seasons'.

Perhaps the last words (for now anyway) can go to Tim Longville. Writing for *Country Life* in 2009 he found himself confronted by the intriguing contrasts of the garden. 'Is it a formal garden of box parterres and geometrical vistas or a woodland garden of lush abundance? Is it a garden designed to display works of art or to show off an array of quirky pieces of topiary? Is it a collection of materials for a botanical artist or a celebration of a half-century of love (and loving difference!) between its creators. The answer is, it is all those things.'

But of course you may be sure there are many more words to come.

Autumn at Shepherd House Garden, the end of the gardening year brings a new beginning.

Acknowledgements

The idea of a book on the garden has been in our minds as a possibility for some time. Knowing nothing of the book business we were a little timid and it would never have happened without the initial encouragement of Fay Young and her husband Ray Perman. Robert Dalrymple was equally enthusiastic. His skill at book design is well known. Our meetings with them were hugely helpful and always fun. Fay managed to bring some sort of order to our initial attempts at writing, always with friendly encouragement. Robert having been bombarded with over 700 photographs patiently selected the best and with his eye for design and layout has created what we hope to be a really special book. When iPads and Kindles are in museums as the artefacts of their generation, fine books skilfully edited and beautifully designed will still grace our bookshelves. If this one is amongst them it will be thanks to Fay and Robert. We are most grateful.

There are more than 200 photographs of the garden in the book, the majority of which are taken by Ann. She describes herself as a garden snapper who can rush out with her camera when the garden is looking at its best. She says (Charlie disagrees) that although she does have an excellent camera, she doesn't have the expertise of the professional.

Since 1991 many professional garden photographers have found their way to Shepherd House. Always welcome, they have become good friends and have been most generous with their photographs. In the early days we were visited by Jerry Harpur, Andrew Lawson and Vivian Russell and later on by Val Corbett, Andrea Jones and Sheila Sim. We are indebted to them all for their permission to use their excellent photographs. All of Ann's paintings in the book have been photographed by Jed Gordon of Musselburgh, who is not only an excellent photographer but who has been most helpful.

Ann's homage to a masterpiece of botanical illustration, Thornton's Temple of Flora: *English Florists' Tulips at Shepherd House.*
18 × 13 INCHES